The Lights Of Leicester Square

Dedication

For my darling daughter and granddaughter, Alexandra and Imogen

The Lights Of Leicester Square

THE GOLDEN YEARS OF CINEMA 1967 TO 1976

Felicity Fair Thompson

Photographs by Harry Myers
Foreword by Michael Grade

Wight Diamond Press

Contents

Acknowledgements

Dear Roy Money, Alan Harris-Quelch, Ted Carter, Roy Pearce...

Walter Hackett, Philip Murphy, Charles Newman, Bill Reid, Charles Duncan, Jeff Cohen, Joe Moody, Chris Hilton...

My sweet friends Dyllis, Rose, Judy, Jackie, Jan, Margaret, Jean, Annie, Eileen, Carol, Eve, Maddie, Marg, Paddy, Olive, Noreen, Dawn, Art, Lynton, Johnny, Ralph, Nick, Philip, Alan, David, Stan, Bill...

Pauline, Shirley, Paddy, Laurie...

How can I put all the names? The list is endless of the wonderful people who worked in the Rank Organisation, in the West End group, and in the Odeon and the Leicester Square Theatres, a kind of 'Cinema Paradiso'. I hope like me, they all remember the lights of Leicester Square in those years with the very greatest pleasure.

★

Thank you to Her Majesty The Queen and TRH the Royal family, who so often graced the red carpet at the Odeon and Leicester Square Theatres over those years and made every occasion so special.

★

Thank you too, to the CTBF in London, and to the hundreds of fabulous film stars and VIPs who brought so much to film and cinema in Leicester Square.

★

Most of all I want to thank Scott Myers and PIC Photographs Ltd for allowing me to use the magic photographs in this book. Scott's father Harry Myers was the constant photographer at all the events and premieres and Royal Film Performances over the time John and I worked in the theatres. Harry was brilliant! He always seemed to be in the right place at the right time - and definitely focussed! He would join us for management social events too, and he was a real pleasure to know. Thank you, Scott, for allowing me to celebrate your father's photographic skills.

Foreword

What is more glamorous than a movie premiere? How many newsreels from Hollywood have we gawped at, seeing the glittering stars of the moving pictures, dressed to the nines, facing the crowds and the photographers before sitting down to watch their latest multimillion dollar production? Well, in the heart of London's West End sits Leicester Square, our equivalent, just as glamorous, just as many searchlights, just as many stars and snappers. Compared to the population of these islands, the crowds packed into Leicester Square on opening nights represent just a tiny, tiny fraction of that number.

BUT luckily, Felicity Fair Thompson had a ringside seat, working at the Odeon Leicester Square, and has put her memories down in print, with some evocative and dazzling photographs of those great nights. It is a labour of love and she gives us all a ringside seat. If you love the movies, you will relish this book over and over again.

Michael Grade
Lord Grade of Yarmouth

—A New Start—

cy cold! It was November 1967. London was far too cold for a young Australian girl more used to Christmas on the beach. I was thin too, a trained ballet dancer, and determined to keep my figure against the freezing odds.

My ballet career though wasn't playing fair. With almost no opportunities for paid work because I'd come back from Europe too late to audition for pantomimes or Christmas specials, I decided to fall back on the old money-making standby, cinema usherette. Working every so often at the Odeon Haymarket between dancing jobs had given me plenty of experience. I knew I could just walk into a job there. I'd been deputy Head Girl so I could probably be Head Girl this time.

I had the job in seconds! Even one in the box office if I'd like that better. 'But,' said the darling manager, Roy Money, 'why don't you go round into Leicester Square? The Odeon there is about to reopen after a fabulous makeover and I know you are just what they want.' I looked at him quizzically. 'Head Receptionist!' he said.

I was interviewed immediately. Leicester Square's handsome General Manager took one look at me as he walked past the interview. 'Take her on,' he said.

And what a place to work! The Rank Organisation had set out to be the best! The West End Rank Cinemas had just been reorganised by the all-powerful Chairman, steely-grey-eyed John Davis. Marble Arch, Haymarket, St Martin's Lane and Kensington were single units. The other cinemas – theatres they were called then, were paired as 'multiple units'. The New Victoria was allied with the Apollo. The Dominion and the Astoria worked as one. The dark towered Odeon in Leicester Square was matched up with Jack Buchanan's lovely old Leicester Square Theatre on the southern side. That was due for a huge revamp too. Leicester Square was definitely the place to be!

—A Glamorous Reception—

The original Odeon had been built for Oscar Deutsch on the site of the glamorous old Alhambra Theatre where the ballerina Anna Pavlova had once danced. For the new 1930s cinema, architect Harry Weedon joined forces with the London Designers Andrew Mather and Thomas Braddock to create the polished black granite building with its huge

Premiere Presentation

of

RONALD COLMAN

in

THE PRISONER
OF ZENDA

Produced by

David O. Selznick

November 2nd
1937

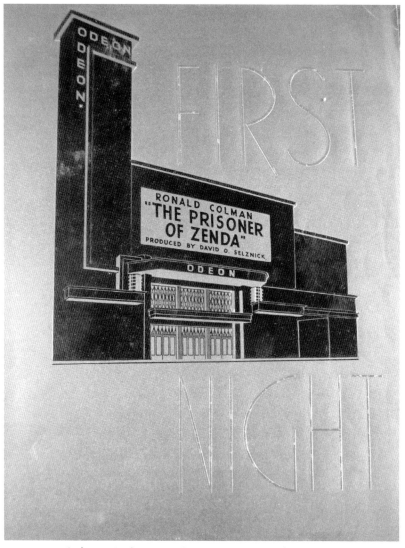

Odeon Leicester Square, November 1937.

lit up advertising space announcing the programme, and with the name of the theatre displayed in descending red florescent letters down the impressive black tower. O D E O N.

The original Odeons were the popular amphitheatres of ancient Greece. That name had been appropriated by France and Italy in the 1920s, but Oscar Deutsch made it his own in Britain. His publicity team insisted the letters stood for Oscar Deutsch Entertains Our Nation!

Inside the auditorium, the seats back then were leopard patterned, and on both of the front side walls were four decorative naked women leaping off wood panelled waves, a design by Raymond Britton Riviere. Rising on cue from the orchestra pit, there was a grand Compton organ, nicknamed the Duchess, the only five keyboard instrument installed in a British cinema. The safety curtain on the full-size theatre stage, and back stage facilities made live performances possible too, as well as showing films.

In 1967 the cost of the make-over was £200,000 in labour costs – approx 3.6 million in today's terms. While the

Compton organ stayed, the four decorative naked women leaping off wood-panelled waves were removed, and this new look Odeon went all red, purple and orange in the foyer carpeting and seating, with salmon pink pseudo fabric on the foyer walls. Sparkling chrome and clear glass were used up the main staircase and for the front of house doors. It was all very shiny and all very new!

If the Odeon had been glamorously made over, it was vital to have staff to match. First of all, the new staff needed training. We all gathered at the Odeon Marble Arch for lessons where *Dr Doolittle* starring Rex Harrison was showing. It was a large auditorium, the perfect place to talk about what was required of us all, and for practising our skills. It wasn't going to be enough just to show people to their seats, or sell them confectionary and ice cream. It all had to be done in style. And it had to be done with an eye to full houses.

At the Odeon Leicester Square there were 1996 seats in the cinema. Sometimes we would be operating on every seat bookable, and sometimes on 'continuous' performance. The latter meant un-numbered seats, and the first come were first served. If there was space on this kind of programming, you could go in late or early and sit right round to when you came in. But there was no allowance for vacant seats. No seat could be wasted, and how to ask people politely to sit down without leaving seats in between mattered. How to get them to move along the row, and do it with manners and style was essential, as was tearing tickets on the door with a smile! Shining your torch on the floor to lead the ticket holders to seats in safely without a hint of a flash in people's eyes was a hard and fast rule – but horror of real horrors, let the beam go anywhere near the screen and you were in real trouble!

Remember the fainting and screaming around the stars you see on newsreels in the 1960s? The Beatles? The Rock stars? The film idols? Because the Odeon Leicester Square was the flagship of the Rank West End cinemas, how to deal with VIP guests and famous movie stars was vital. Of course the staff rule was decorum, and never to even contemplate asking for autographs! Some of the girls really had to be talked round on that idea!

The opening in December was looming. There were to be twelve men with a Chief of Staff in charge of them. As Head Receptionist I would be responsible for over forty girls working on rotas, their time off, their breaks, their uniforms and their appearance, their holidays, and their time-keeping. On duty they had to staff the exits and entrances, show people to seats, and be available for intermission sales, and cloakroom duties. And it all had to be perfect. We had to be like First Class air hostesses and stewards.

We were measured up for uniforms, all designer wear and very smart. For the girls: a grey dress and jacket with green silk trimmings, with short fashionable sixties' hemlines of course. For the men: a grey suit with green silk lapels. The Link men, as the chaps who were going to park cars were called, had capes and caps as well. We all wore white cotton gloves! Gloves, no less! Everyone looked so good. The girls were given black mid-heel court shoes, and a hair allowance to get a hairdo before the important re-opening night. The boys got crisp white shirts. We all felt we were special. I just knew I had stepped into a new and very exciting world.

—A Breathtaking Beginning—

West End Style.

Before the opening we had staff rehearsals. The most important of these was a complete and detailed fire drill, including clearing the theatre in case of any emergency. We spent two hours going over what might happen, how it would happen, and who was responsible for what. I found it quite breath-taking! Listening to the official announcement from the stage that the theatre had to be cleared, and looking round the huge auditorium, and knowing all my girls and if necessary, the male staff too, had to listen to my instructions and follow my lead, I wondered what on earth I thought I was doing taking this job! There would be just short of two thousand people to be shown out safely, quickly and efficiently, plus I needed to take responsibility for the safety of all the staff. It was a daunting idea. I had a wonderful deputy, Dyllis, from Wales. I remember looking over at her and making a face! She smiled back. That was so encouraging. We would stick together. I knew we would be fine.

Headline news.

The cinema opened on 28th December 1967 with Lynn Redgrave and Rita Tushingham in *Smashing Time.*

Though some mourned the modernisation, particularly the loss of the leaping figures that had adorned the side walls, the *Evening Standard* front page headline announced: 'It's the New Look Odeon Leicester Sq' – and continued on: 'The black monolithic Odeon, the brooding Leicester Square memorial to Oscar Deutsch, Birmingham metal-maker turned cinema magnate, glitters anew.'

My girls were all lined up at their right positions. Outside the Square was crowded with hundreds and hundreds of fans. The red carpet was out. The General Manager and his Deputy were on the Front of House greeting the stars, and Cliff Richard and the Shadows were going to open the evening with a live stage show. The famous faces included the stars of the film, Lynn Redgrave and Rita Tushingham, and Richard Attenborough, Sandie Shaw, Terence Stamp, Adam Faith, and the Redgrave family. The film was an odd and rather parochial one I thought, for such a prestigious opening night, but it was British. And with

Crowds gathering for opening night.

the Royal Film Performance due on 4th March, there were much more exciting times to come.

One thing we girls discovered that very first night: our new black court shoes were lethal! Not high or ill fitting, but alive with electricity when combined with the nylon content of the theatre's new carpet. Every time we touched any chrome fitting or the chrome stair rails, we all got shock after shock after shock! It certainly would keep us on our toes!

—Our First Royal Film Performance—

Royal Film Performance 1968
in the gracious presence of
Her Majesty The Queen
to aid the Cinema and Television Benevolent Fund

March 1968 – Franco Zeffirelli's wonderful *Romeo and Juliet*. There was to be a stage show as well as the film. The theatre was closed on the Sunday so that stage rehearsals could take place. The upstairs foyer was set up briefly with dining tables to serve a silver service lunch. The evening's stars included Juliet, sixteen-year-old Olivia Hussey, and Romeo, seventeen-year-old Leonard Whiting, the film Director himself, Franco Zeffirelli, and Elizabeth Taylor and Richard Burton, Christopher Plummer, Mia Farrow, Tommy Steele, Karl Malden, Joanna Pettet, Lynn Redgrave, David Hemmings, Olinka Berova, Richard Chamberlain, Joan Colllins, Danny Robin, Topol, Peter Ustinov, Susannah York, Carol White and Danny Kaye. Richard Attenborough was to compere the stage show.

All of them and more were due to be in the Royal 'line-up', and closed-circuit television presented by Rediffusion would be beamed from the circle foyer into the auditorium, so all other guests could be ushered in to their seats. They would certainly be keen to watch everything happening on the screen. Later the highlights were edited into a transmission for ITV. You can still see film from that evening on YouTube March 4th 1968. The arrival areas were packed with beautifully dressed people, star spotting, and being seen themselves on their way in to take their seats, but only those with an enclosure pass could remain outside

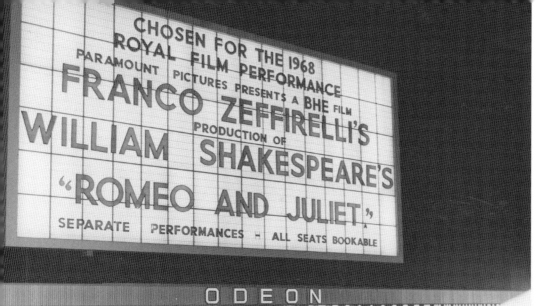

CHOSEN FOR THE 1968
ROYAL FILM PERFORMANCE
PARAMOUNT PICTURES PRESENTS A BHE FILM
FRANCO ZEFFIRELLI'S
WILLIAM SHAKESPEARE'S
PRODUCTION OF
"ROMEO AND JULIET"
SEPARATE PERFORMANCES - ALL SEATS BOOKABLE

ODEON

Paramount Pictures presents a BHE Film.
Franco Zeffirelli's production of William Shakespeare's
'Romeo & Juliet'

The 1968
Royal Film
Performance

*Her Majesty The Queen is introduced to the stars including Tommy Steele,
Joan Collins, Richard Chamberlain, Susannah York and Karl Malden.*

Danny Kaye and Peter Ustinov watch Leonard Whiting, Romeo, and Olivia Hussey, Juliet, meeting the Duke of Edinburgh.

been utterly terrified in case anything went wrong, and had each had a good shot of vodka!

I had to be out in the upstairs foyer as well, to make sure the cloakrooms were closed before the line-up introductions

the auditorium. The foyers needed to be clear for the Royal arrivals. From inside the circle on that closed circuit screening, while I was checking all was well with the staff, I remember seeing John Thompson, the General Manager, and Walter Hackett, his deputy, looking very confident as they waited by the red carpet for the royal cars to arrive. Later when I knew him better, John told me they had both

So many famous faces in the line-up – Topol, Joanna Pettet, Karl Malden, Lynn Redgrave, David Hemmings and Richard Attenborough.

began, and that the staff members were in their right places there, and to encourage people into the auditorium because they could see it all on the screen – so I was seeing things close up. The Queen was there with the Duke of Edinburgh, and at his first Royal Film Performance, so was Prince Charles, moving slowly and nervously along the line-up of people to be introduced. He certainly took more time at it than the Queen and the Duke, who were old hands at the game.

I was passed the Royal party's stoles and evening coats to pop in the cloakroom. 'Ooooh,' the girls whispered, smelling them for perfume, and hanging them up carefully. 'Hey! This one has a hole! Can you believe it?' It wasn't the Queen's, and it was only a minute hole, but it was there!

The bouquets were presented and inside the auditorium, the trumpeters filed on stage in their gold and red outfits and the fanfare was played as the Queen entered. She swept into the royal box which had been installed overnight in the front circle with carpeted platform, glamorous gold seats, with red upholstery and gold trimmings, and all surrounded with fresh flowers. The national anthem sounded. First there was a loyal address by Richard Attenborough to welcome Her Majesty. Then the grand red tabs swept aside and the stage show began. The occasion was regarded as one of the most successful evenings ever organised by the Cinema and Television Benevolent Fund, raising an all-time record at the time of £36,850 (nearly £550,000 today) for the Charity. I hurried up the back stairs and into the rear circle and watched briefly. But once the film began, I had to tear myself away from it. I had staff duties to worry about – breaks and positions, and cloakroom duties, and staff line-ups for afterwards. Everything that evening went off perfectly

and we all breathed a sigh of relief when the Queen's car departed from the front of house doors, all the exits were finally closed and locked, and the theatre shut for the night.

Day to day organising of the staff rota took time. Full-time staff worked one weekend in three, and there were part-time weekend and evening staff as well. The theatre was open seven days a week and there had to be the right number of staff on at any one time. Fire and safety regulations dictated that. It was also important that everyone's uniform continued looking ultra smart. So there was washing to do! And those white gloves had to be very white!

If there was an intermission, there were sales to be made. Rose, a fellow Australian, ran the 'Ice room'. Redhead Rose was delightful. She organised her stock and sales very effectively, but with her dry humour, she was very good fun to work with too. The receptionists had to wear an orange smock dress over their uniforms, have individual floats to be able to give change, and have plenty of 'parfait' ice-creams to sell from their ice-cream trays. The 'parfait' was delicious, with layers of cream and ice-cream and fruit purée – as good as any dessert in a smart West End restaurant. For sales, the girls had to be ready for intermissions at the back of the stalls to go down the aisle to be near the stage, or in the circle, to stand near the wall on either side to give room for a queue, or step down the front circle steps to the front where they could easily be seen by all of the upstairs audience. And of course, there was a sales kiosk in the entrance foyer, and a licensed bar in the upstairs foyer. Those sales staff had to be ready for intermission business, and for before and between the performances too.

John Thompson the General Manager had a real eye for selling, and was keen to keep up his winning record. There was an amazing two weeks where he persuaded me to dress up as a Dutch girl and sell Dutch chocolates to the queues in the foyer who were waiting to buy their tickets from the central box office cubical, and then who would go on slowly into the stalls, or up the stairs to the circle. I'm quite good at talking to people, and in that fortnight, it was a very rare individual who escaped into the auditorium without those chocolates! John Thompson won the Rank cinema's national prize for the most sales, and we broke all the records. He was given a weekend away in Holland, and I received a watch! It was tricky keeping up with staffing in that fortnight, and in the dressing room the girls found it a huge joke to have a Dutch chocolate girl as the boss, but it was amusing stomping around in clogs, the wide skirt, and a Dutch hat with its triangular shape with wings – and the selling was certainly successful!

And the big films kept coming. The Duke of Edinburgh attended *The Charge of the Light Brigade* in April 1968 – some amazing actors were in this Tony Richardson film: Leslie Howard, Vanessa Redgrave, John Gielgud, Harry Andrews, Jill Bennett and David Hemmings. I can remember David Hemmings coming in to several subsequent performances and standing watching, leaning on the wall at the back of the Stalls.

—Moving Up – Who's that girl?—

By May 1968 my name was being used for advertising! In the Evening Standard an ad appeared in the General Vacancies column: 'WHY NOT JOIN FELICITY KINMONT AT THE ODEON LEICESTER SQUARE? She is Australian, she is young and keen and very happy at her work. She needs young attractive girls for full-time positions to help her in the seating and selling duties at London's Premiere Theatre. Five-day week, rotating weekends and the best rates of pay in the business.'
Come and Join Felicity.

In July 1968 a short article about 'School for Usherettes' appeared in *The Times*, and then a more detailed article by Marilyn Cunningham appeared in the *Daily Sketch*. Photos were taken, Marilyn interviewed me, and her article was headlined NOW, A TOUCH OF STYLE IN THE AISLES... 'Just in case you didn't know it, there's a lot more to being a cinema usherette than simply showing the customers to their seats. So much more in fact, that one of Britain's most luxurious cinemas – the newly refurbished Odeon in London's Leicester Square – has started a special training school for its staff.' And there was picture of me at a blackboard with four of the girls, captioned: 'Felicity Kinmont: bringing a change to the cinema.'

In Leicester Square there was certainly much more to being a Receptionist, as usherettes were called now. It was definitely like being a short flight air hostess in First Class, and the men were certainly like the First Class flight attendants. Working in a glamorous environment really did mean maintaining high standards.

It was just after this that the General Manager John Thompson asked me if I would like to join the management. I had been thinking that I might go back to Australia, but I did know how exciting the Odeon could be. He reminded me that the Leicester Square Theatre on the southern side of the Square was about to be totally refurbished, and he explained that when it re-opened, it and the Odeon would be running as a 'Multiple Unit'. The management and staff would operate both theatres in tandem. He needed someone like me as Assistant Manager he said, to make it work, and Deputy Head Receptionist Dyllis who knew my current job through and through would step up as Head Receptionist. Dyllis was such a sweet friend. She would be brilliant, I knew that. The film *Oliver* was due to open in September at the Odeon. There were good things ahead.

So now I was on the management! And I was quite impressed to be the very first woman Front of House Manager to work in the West End for Rank. Yes, there were women in charge of box offices, and secretaries to the Area Controllers, and women on the office management in cinemas around the country, but I was the first woman to be so directly dealing with the film audiences and cinema goers for Rank in London's West End.

Daily Sketch, July 6, 1968.

Top left: Mark Lester with Lulu and
Lionel Bart.
Bottom left: Ron Moody and Leo Jaffe.
Above: Shani Wallace – Nancy in the film – with
her husband Bernie Rich.

Left: Danny La Rue.
Right: Mark Lester with his proud parents.
Below: Hayley Mills and Roy Boulting.

Douglas Fairbanks.

Sept 26th 1968. *Oliver* was a spectacular premier! Princess Margaret and Antony Armstrong-Jones came, and so did Prime Minister Harold Wilson and his wife. Mark Lester and Jack Wild were doing the presentations of flowers and a special book to the Princess and her husband. Lionel Bart came. So did Richard Attenborough. Ron Moody, the wonderful Fagin was there. And Douglas Fairbanks. So were Danny La Rue, Lulu, Shani Wallis, and Hayley Mills and Roy Boulting – and many others. So many famous faces. Not even Oliver could have asked for more! And now I was out in the Foyer as a manager, wearing the long black velvet dress I had made myself for the occasion, helping to move the crowds into the auditorium, and when it came to the moment, guiding the two boys from the film, Mark and Jack, who were strangely nervous presenters of the bouquet and gift, to step forward and do the presentation to Princess Margaret and Antony Armstrong-Jones after the princess and her husband had been around the line-up of stars, the film's directors, and the producers.

Making my own dresses was going to become more and more important. One needed to keep up with the glamour, a costly pursuit of course, and it was the late sixties, and London was zinging with style! My capacity for sewing was proving useful. In earlier times when I had worked as a dancer, a 'Blue Coat', and with the children's entertainers, for a summer season for Pontins Holiday Camp in Lowestoft, I was making two new dresses a week for the female vocalist! Now for the constant premieres in Leicester Square, I could make a dress for myself with glamorous sleeves and wear it, and then take out the sleeves and wear it sleeveless the next time. Then I could make a kind of full-length waistcoat layer in slightly different material and wear that over the dress! But black after black was boring. The one time I actually bought an evening dress from famous old Swan and Edgar at Piccadilly Circus and cheekily didn't opt for managerial black, the steely-eyed Chairman John Davis pointed me out at the premiere and asked 'Who is that woman in white?!' I was being noticed!

Above: Harold and Mary Wilson, Jack Wilde and
Mark Lester.
Top right: Princess Margaret greets
Mrs Virginia Ogilvy.
Bottom right: Antony Armstrong-Jones receives
the official Oliver Souvenir Programme.

Mark Lester and Jack Wilde present flowers to Princess Margaret.

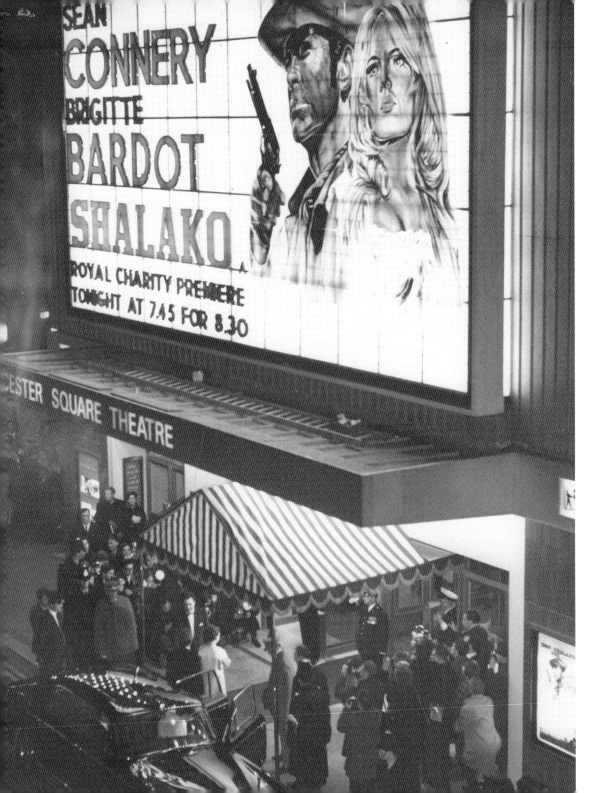

—On the Double—

The next high point was the re-opening of the Leicester Square Theatre on December 11th, 1968. The film was *Shalako* with Sean Connery and Brigitte Bardot. It took £12,945 in its first week, the equivalent in 2020 of £226,000! Princess Margaret came to the opening, as always looking very beautiful. And Jack Hawkins, Stephan Boyd, Chips Rafferty, Richard Attenborough, and many others were there. There were always stars.

The Leicester Square Theatre was very different in design from the Odeon. Once a live theatre, built for Jack Buchanan, it had stalls, a circle and a balcony. Now the circle was outlined with concealed lighting troughs, giving the impression it was suspended in space. With the modernisation, the layout had been kept, though the theatre organ there was removed, as was the balcony. There was green seating for 1402, and green carpet. It all felt very green! Everywhere in the foyers, shiny green tiled walls reflected the light. Across the Square the Odeon had red as its main colour.

The Leicester Square Theatre re-opens December 1968.

Now we were operating a truly Multiple Unit. With another fourteen hundred seats in the LST as we called it now, and twenty minutes separating opening times, it was important to make sure staff members were shared between the two theatres, using maximum numbers as one house went in, and then leaving just the required number of staff behind on duty to comply with fire and safety regulations. We could take the extra staff across the Square to help with seating and sales. With intermission sales too, again it was possible to share staff numbers. This also applied to management, so it would mean darting across the Square after seeing the Odeon house in, to be available on Front of House in the Leicester Square Theatre to see that audience in too – and back and forth for intermissions and seeing the house out. It was all really exciting and very, very hectic!

I remember sorting out a double booking: agency V theatre box office and having a kind letter from David English of Associated

HRH Princess Margaret arrives for the Premiere of Shalako.

Top left: Good evening, Ma'am!
Above: Jack Hawkins looks on as Princess Margaret meets Stephan Boyd.
Left: Stephan Boyd, Brigitte Bardot, Sean Connery.
Right: Brigitte Bardot meets Antony Armstrong Jones while Sean Connery talks to Princess Margaret.

Richard Attenborough with wife Sheila Sim and daughter Charlotte.

Newspapers Evening News, thanking me for helping him and his family sort out some difficulties with their tickets. 'It was very refreshing to be able to talk to somebody who is so polite and efficient.' We always had such interesting theatre-goers and it was great to receive a lovely letter from such a well-known British journalist and newspaper editor! It made me feel I was in the right job!

Meanwhile *Oliver* was winning all sorts of awards. In the Academy Awards John Woolf won for Best Picture and Carol Reed won Best Director. Shepperton Studios won Best Sound, and an Honorary Award for Choreography went to Onna White. Not surprising! The dance scenes were wonderful. More awards and nominations followed in the Golden Globes and Baftas. Ron Moody won award after award for Best Actor, and young Jack Wild as the Artful Dodger was recognised as the most promising newcomer to leading film roles. The film gave me particular pleasure because when I was briefly in London as a youngster, I had seen the staged musical on its very first night at the London Palladium years before. It was a runaway success then! Now the film was too. It ran at the Odeon for over thirteen weeks then moved across to the Leicester Square Theatre where it went on doing wonderful business.

Chitty Chitty Bang Bang was shown at the Odeon for one glamorous night on 16th December 1968 with the Queen, Prince Phillip, Prince Charles and Princess Anne in attendance. Vintage cars and Royalty! It was the biggest ever world premiere, held simultaneously in eleven other cities, with the Royal party's arrival and interviews with the stars relayed by television land lines to each cinema and projected onto the screen before the start of the film. It transferred to the Astoria in Charing Cross Road for its run.

1968 had been a strange year. In April Martin Luther King was assassinated, and then Bobby Kennedy in June. There were riots in Paris in May, Russian tanks rolling into Prague in August, and street battles in Londonderry in October. Richard Nixon became US President in the November, and astronauts orbited the moon for the first time that December.

Overleaf: HM The Queen greeted by John Thompson, and : Flowers for Her Majesty. Model car for the Duke.

A very royal evening: Princess Anne and Prince Charles. and: James Callaghan Home Secretary looks on as the Duke admires his special gift.

—Working in the Heart of Town—

London's West End was amazing then. Though it was crowded, the Square was still a beautifully kept garden in the centre, with a statue of William Shakespeare, surrounded on all four sides by the road. Beside the Odeon, near the box office on the south side of what in theatre terms was the 'front of house', there was an alleyway, part of the Odeon premises. The queues to buy tickets, often five people abreast, stretched through that alleyway, then north up Charing Cross Road, then left into Bear Street, and back around into Leicester Square, right to the theatre's front of house doors at the north end. Once the queue reached there, one really needed to discourage people from joining it. They certainly wouldn't get in! When there was a record-breaking film on, there would be that long queue, plus another couple of thousand people in the Square, hoping to join the queue, and then inside the theatre, there would be nearly two thousand people already watching the movie!

I remember one occasion being on duty as manager in the main Odeon foyer, and we had just opened the rope stanchions for the very large queue to divide and move into the foyer to each side of the central ticket box. Continuous performance tickets were sold like that – buy your ticket and go straight into the auditorium – via the kiosk, or the upstairs Licensed Bar of course! Suddenly someone from much further back in the line tried to jump the queue, stepping out and pushing roughly past others to get to the ticket desk. All these people had lined up around the block

for ages, and they certainly weren't in the mood for someone breaking the rules of polite British queuing! A rumpus broke out! There was nothing for it. I leapt up several steps of the circle staircase, took a deep breath, and raised my voice. 'Stop selling tickets!' The box office girls in the ticket box froze. The crowd started to go quiet. 'Quiet please!' Everyone looked up at me. 'QUIET!' The foyer was silent.

'Now, there will be no more tickets sold until you all settle down, and the gentleman who tried to jump the queue steps aside.' Everyone turned to the culprit. He looked around angrily at his accusers. I went down the steps and straight to him. 'I'm sorry but you can't come in. These queues have to proceed in an orderly fashion." He stared at me as if I was mad. I held my ground. 'I am the Theatre Manager, and I reserve the right to say who comes into this theatre and who doesn't!' A couple of people cheered! The man glanced round. 'She's right,' said someone. 'Where's the Manager,' he said. 'I am the Manager,' I said. Another cheer. He looked me up and down. 'You?' I nodded. He hesitated. I stood up straighter. He opened his mouth to say something else, then gave me a nasty look and turned and strode angrily out the door. A big cheer. 'Start selling again,' I said to the girls. They grinned at me and began issuing tickets again. The queue was much calmer now, and of course it turned into another full house!

To entertain the long queues, in those days there were street entertainers out in the Square. Buskers they were called. They played to the crowds and earned a good living providing amazing entertainment while people waited. There were singers, and clowns, and jugglers, and one particular man who was a walking orchestra! He played an accordion, and he had a mouth organ, and a flute, and then there was a washboard strapped to the top of his back with some kind of mechanism for scraping it up and down, a drum strapped on his lower back he could operate with his upper arms, and he had cymbals somewhere too with a connecting string he operated by stamping his foot. I think he also had a banjo, but I can't quite remember how he could play that as well! He certainly kept the queues amused!

In the mid winter at the Square end of the alley, there was a man with a stove, cooking chestnuts for the crowds. Some time later John Thompson decided to install an ice-cream stall in the alley too. That was very popular, and not just in the summer, but all year round!

The road round Leicester Square was closed for premieres and Charity performances when the Queen or members of the Royal family came from Buckingham Palace or Clarence House. The Royal car would bring them along the Mall, round Trafalgar Square, into Charing Cross Road, and turn left along Bear Street and into Leicester Square to the front doors of the Odeon. They would step out onto the lush red carpet, which had been rolled out from the centre doors across the pavement and onto the road to exactly where the car would draw up.

There would be crowd barriers all along our side of the Square and gardens, to keep back the crowds who had come to see the Royal guests and the film stars arrive. Sometimes, there would be marching bands in the Square, and sometimes something particularly appropriate for the film, like the wonderful cars there had been for *Chitty Chitty Bang Bang*. The huge hoarding display screen across the front of the theatre was always lit up with the film advertising. Even the hundreds of starlings in the trees in the Gardens would be singing!

In the mornings Leicester Square was an utterly different place. The day started at 10 a.m. for me, and going across the road to the National Westminster Bank on the south side of the Square, there would be hardly anyone about. Maybe one person, or two. Interestingly last thing every night, whoever was Duty Manager, and that was often me, would go over the road with a kind of locked brown leather pouch with the takings inside. It could easily be more than a thousand pounds. At the bank there was a Night Safe. With a key to unlock that, you popped the leather pouch in, pushed the safe door shut again, and heard the pouch fall. In the morning it was necessary to go and sign that money in, and sometimes pay in other money. I always carried that pouch or pay-in money in some kind of shopping bag, or in my handbag, or in some 'ordinary' way, to attract the least attention. Any manager doing this night time banking was instructed that if stopped, we were not to stand our ground. 'Just pass the money over,' John Thompson said to us. 'You're more important than takings.'

Mornings inside the theatres could be very busy. When there was a new film due, there would be a Press Show so that journalists could view the film in advance of it showing, and do their write-ups for the newspapers and magazines, to be printed with the photographs of the event in the following morning's editions. There was a beautiful room under the Odeon stalls foyer known as the Royal Retiring Room, with pale comfortable sofas around the edge, and decorated with lots of mirrors and subtle lighting. That would be set up as a bar for premieres, but used for morning

There were always crowds in Leicester Square to see the stars.

Press Shows too. The members of the Press came down there after seeing the film to talk to each other, compare ideas, and chat over a few drinks or coffee before setting off back to their newspaper offices.

That early time of day could also have another excitement. When there was going to be a big boxing match on at Wembley, the Boxing stars came to be weighed in at the Odeon. There would a set of scales centre stage in front of the gold secondary curtains, with the main red curtains drawn back, and the boxing managers, promoters, organisers and press photographers all there to witness the weigh-ins, as they were called. If a Boxing star was slightly above their advertised weight, they would go in behind our huge advertising hoarding, which was behind a screen and curtained off from the circle foyer, where they could run up and down in the heat of all the hundreds of light bulbs to achieve the right weight! As a woman manager I was not allowed to witness this or the staged weigh-ins, just in case a boxer had to take off a piece of clothing to achieve the perfect weight! Might it be his shorts? I might only have been watching the procedure from the back stalls anyway – hardly a close-up view, and I found it really amusing to be barred from these moments! Nobody minded me there on the front of house though, to show the press inside the stalls for these weigh-ins!

Morning was the time in the theatres to check the staff levels for the day, and do the necessary bookwork. At that time wages were worked out on site and the staff members were paid in cash – the little brown envelopes had totals of money earned for the week, and what tax and National Insurance had been paid. The cleaning in both buildings had to be checked too – if in between and under the rows of seats had been thoroughly swept, if all the chrome had been beautifully polished, how well all the carpets had been vacuumed, if all the toilets had been properly cleaned.

There was an amazing moment just before the Leicester Square Theatre closed for its refurbishment, when it was discovered that a lady, who was not a member of staff, had been running the ladies toilets for years. She arrived every day apparently, and worked all day in there, taking money for showing the ladies into the toilets, and keeping the cubicles and hand washing facilities in good order. No-one knew she was even there, but apparently she must have made enough money out of the tips for it to be worthwhile doing!

In the Odeon there was a darling old East End lady called Annie who was part of the cleaning staff. She was always smiling and reliable, and anxious to please, and I loved the way she worked with such energy and enjoyment. She was skinny and agile and had fun vacuuming really fast and well. If she found the slightest patch of dust, she was down on her knees sorting it, and she was always jumping about to get the place absolutely spotless. She worked six nights a week, and she was far and away the best cleaner the theatre had. I was really sad when a couple of years into my time at the Odeon, it was discovered that Annie was in her late eighties! Of course, it wasn't possible given the employment laws for her to go on working in the theatre, and she was given her notice. But when she left, we really missed her!

Leicester Square is surrounded by Art. In Charing Cross Road is the National Portrait Gallery, and in Trafalgar Square, the National Gallery. Towards Soho, in Leicester Place, I discovered the Roman Catholic church of Notre Dame de France, with its roots dating back to the French revolution. There's the wonderful Aubusson tapestry created by a Benedictine monk, Dom Robert, and the building, damaged by bombs in the Second World War, was given new life in 1959 with the marvellous murals in the Lady Chapel painted by Jean Cocteau, who, it was said, lit a candle at the feet of the statue of Our Lady of Lourdes before beginning work every day, and talked constantly to his biblical characters as he painted them.

Working in Leicester Square meant I had to do my shopping locally, and the place for fruit and vegetables was definitely Berwick Street market. Walking up Wardour Street from the Square, along Shaftesbury Avenue, and turning into narrow little Rupert Street, in summer I could smell the fresh strawberries even before I passed through the alley of strip clubs and bars, and emerged into the market. What a place! Stalls! Street sellers! Tiny shops all along the edge. And the freshest vegetables and fruit you could ever see, with a wonderful sound track of trading calls and marketing! I could have been on the set in *Oliver*!

At the north end of it was Oxford Street, and my favourite department store, Bourne and Hollingsworth – lovely fashion, good fabrics, cosmetics – everything! And from there I could walk along to Oxford Circus, and down Regent Street to Liberty. Their fabrics were to die for! So was the building! That beautiful Tudor facade is still there, and inside, so is the central hall with the galleried floors above it – it was worth me wanting to buy fabric just to go there. Nearby John Lewis was wonderful for material in those days

too. Back then more people were interested in making and sewing things themselves. Then of course there was Carnaby Street which was always crowded with skinny girls in mini skirts and wide-eyed make up. That was a place to be seen! And to see posters and advertising with Jean Shrimpton and Twiggy everywhere. At the other end of Regent Street, near Piccadilly Circus, was the very classy Fortnum and Mason, which is still there of course, but Swan and Edgar, right on the Circus roundabout has gone. That was a wonderful department store too. Piccadilly Circus itself was beautiful with its central statue of Eros, and all the advertising and lighting, and the red buses – true London! And just a short walk from more of true London – Leicester Square.

—Presentation—

World Premieres, British Premieres, the annual Royal Film Performance in the presence of the Queen or the Queen Mother, which early on included a staged variety show... Charity performances, solo runs of the very best films for up to six weeks without any competition – it was an amazing place to be working, and to be right in there amongst the stars.

Barbra Streisand was definitely a star and a Funny Girl. In January 1969 she and Omar Sharif came to the Odeon for the Royal Charity premiere of this wonderful film. It was a busy night and Streisand looked utterly terrified on arrival. Along with her own minders for protection, she seemed to need to be encircled by management as well. As one of these managers, I was amazed that such a star could feel so threatened by the people in the foyers. She was visibly shaking with fear. It certainly wasn't from the cold. She was very warmly dressed in a fur collared coat and fur hat, and she looked wonderful.

We sheltered her up the staircase to the circle foyer, and there, standing waiting in the line-up next to Omar Sharif, she did begin to relax a little. Princess Margaret was due, and as usual the main audience had to be ushered inside, leaving just the stars, the film producers, and executives for the line-up. As usual the Royal arrival and greeting the

Barbra Streisand.
Overleaf: Funny Girl January 1969;
Barbra Streisand and Omar Sharif.

guests was all being filmed anyway and beamed onto the screen inside the auditorium.

The Princess arrived, came up the staircase, and made her way round the line-up. When she reached him, of course she talked enthusiastically to Omar Sharif, and then before moving on, turned back to him for that moment too long – well, we all would! Meanwhile next to him, Streisand's careful bow was totally missed. She looked quite miffed. Margaret, still in conversation with Sharif, then turned back to Streisand. The princess smiled and shook hands, spoke to her briefly, and then progressed on almost immediately to collect the bouquet from Camilla Harmsworth, the little girl I was ready to manoeuvre forward.

Streisand turned masterfully away to talk to others as if none of it mattered anyway. It was a strange lesson in pride I thought – almost terror to start with at being so famous, and then throw-away carelessness when she wasn't really concentrated on. It must be quite challenging being a celebrity!

Left: Camilla Harmsworth presents the bouquet to Princess Margaret.
Below: Barbra Streisand, Omar Sharif and Princess Margaret.
Right: The Royal Film Performance, February 1969.

A string of wonderful films followed in 1969. *The Prime of Miss Jean Brodie* starring Maggie Smith and Robert Stephens was the Royal Film Performance in February with the Queen Mother, Princess Margaret, Princess Alexandra, and Prince Michael of Kent attending.

Above: Ron Moody.
Right: It's an exciting night for the three children. David Livingstone has presented the first bouquet to HM The Queen Mother.

There were three little children with bouquets for me to guide forward that night, Samantha Parkins, David Livingstone, and Marc Samuelson.

The evening raised a huge £36,680 for the Cinema and Television Benevolent Fund, (£650,500 in 2020). The pipes and drums of the First Battalion, the Scots Guards marched in the Square, and stars included Sir Michael Redgrave, Roger Moore, Warren Mitchell, Nyree Dawn Porter, Ron Moody, Melina Mercuri, Ava Gardner, Rachel Roberts, Peter Sellers and Rex Harrison.

Above: Rex Harrison and Ava Gardner with Antony Armstrong Jones, and Peter Sellers.
Left: Marc Samuelson presents the bouquet to Princess Margaret.
Right: Princess Alexandra receives her bouquet from Samantha Parkins.

Left Royal Premiere McKenna's Gold April 1969.
Top right: Omar Sharif and Camilla Sparv.
Far right: Guiding the little bouquet presenter forward.
Overleaf left: Princess Margaret and Antony Armstrong-Jones. See? It's fun talking to royalty.
Overleaf right: Princess Anne attends the Premiere of Run Wild Run Free, March 1969.

Circle

Sea

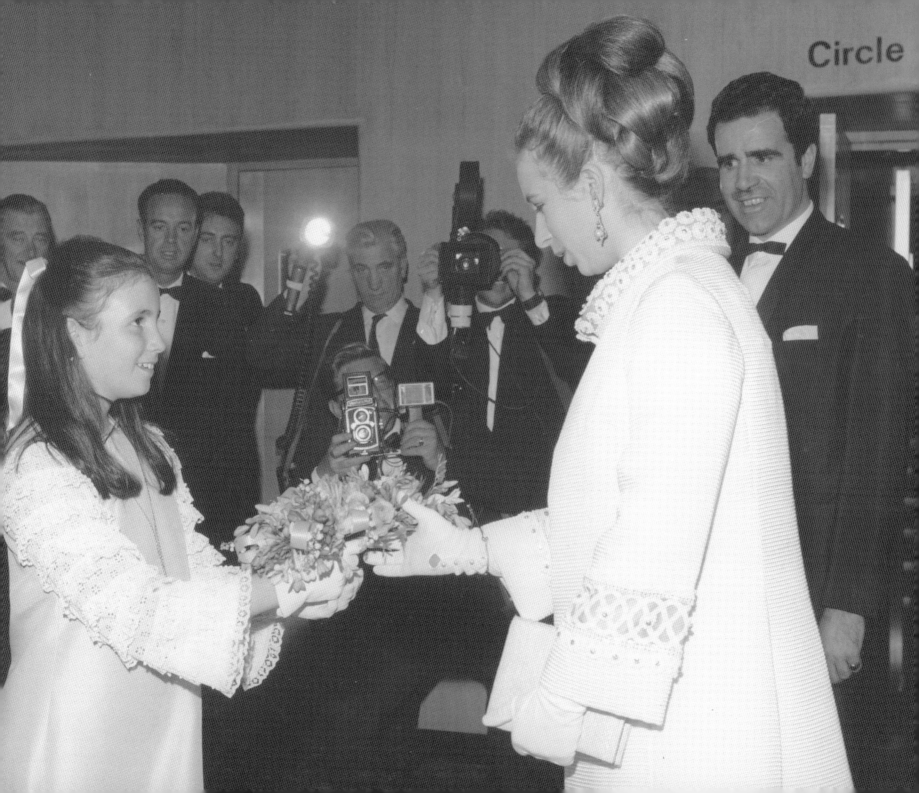

Greeting stars is all in her day's work

FELICITY Kinmont puts her feet up at the end of a working day, and recalls the stars she has met.

For greeting showbusiness personalities is all in a day's work for Felicity, at 22 an assistant manager of two of London's biggest cinemas—the Leicester-square Theatre and the Odeon, Leicester-square, which is the scene of a glittering royal premiere several times a year.

"The guest list on such occasions reads like a 'Who's Who' of showbusiness, and when I write home recounting how Rolf Harris wise-cracked with me, how Robert Stevens winked, or how Bill Travers introduced his wife, Virginia McKenna, it is difficult not to name drop," explains Miss Kinmont, whose home is in Sydney, Australia.

She has been with the Rank Organisation since shortly after her arrival in this country four years ago.

On other side

Miss Kinmont, whose looks rival those of many of the glamorous personalities she greets, began her career on the other side of showbusiness.

"I came to England to pursue my career as a dancer," she explains " but after a few months in London I realised that for most of my profession, six months' work a year was the most to hope for. Preferring to be fully employed I went along to the Odeon Leicester-square and obtained a job as head receptionist."

Felicity qualified for this comparatively senior appointment by explaining that during a previous period of professional "resting" she had worked at another West End Odeon, rising to the position of female receptionist supervisor.

She found work at the Odeon, Leicester-square so fascinating that she joined the permanent staff, and in January of this year she was promoted to assistant manager, in charge of 150 staff—two-thirds of them women.

Responsibility

Asked the secret of her speedy rise to a challenging position as such a young age, Felicity said: "I think it is the same in the cinema world as in most professions; you prove yourself by successfully taking big responsibilities and handling other staff without constantly bothering your superiors for advice.

"Handling large numbers of staff is the biggest part of the challenge when you are young, but we are fortunate that the Odeon's policy is to employ young people and with the exception of our cleaners, none of the staff is over 30."

Staff are recruited for their looks, grooming and personality, as well as for their professional ability and enthusiasm for the job.

14-hour day

"Torch drill is only one aspect," she said. "In addition to lessons on grooming and makeup, the girls are taught the correct way to sell ices and refreshments. They are also taught how to tackle a vast variety of inquiries.

The order of what is often a 14-hour day for Felicity has the variety of a patch-work quilt, and requires a similar attention to detail.

Hours of duty usually span from 1 p.m. until 11 p.m. and involve checks in every part of the 2,000-seater cinemas to ensure that all areas are in tip-top conditions for the public.

The afternoon may see Felicity translating for a Parisian visiting his first London cinema. The end of the day will certainly see her checking all aspects of the day's take and finalising security arrangements.

Preparations

The glitter of a royal premiere can only take place if it is preceded by exhaustive behind - the-scenes preparations.

On the morning itself, the cinema is awake at 7 a.m. Felicity and her colleagues are making a microscopic check on every part of the cinema—from light switches in the toilets to ash trays in the retiring room; haute cuisine catering arrangements are completed; barrier ropes set in place, thousands of flowers received and arranged; bouquets for presentation stored carefully in their required chilled conditions.

Programmes arrive; the red carpet is rolled out; zero hour approaches. The cinema hums with finishing-touch activity and suppressed excitement An immaculate staff with newly-coiffured hair is lined up for head-to-toe inspection.

The guests of honour enter to a fanfare of trumpets, and as Felicity expertly guides some small protegee in presentation of the bouquet, she receives the gracious smile and kind remark that makes every moment of preparation worthwhile.

Sweet Charity came on at the end of the same month and was heralded as a sweet success. Next was *Ring of Bright Water*, and that was followed by *McKenna's Gold*.

Then came *Run Wild Run Free*, starring John Mills and Mark Lester who had played Oliver, with Princess Anne as the Royal guest, her first time on her own.

And at the Leicester Square Theatre there was a morning premiere of *Lionheart* to celebrate the Silver Jubilee of children's films for the Children's Film Foundation.

There was a feature about me in the *Torquay Herald Express*.

And something else was happening in my life. John Thompson and I were getting to know each other better. Standing on the front of house talking to me began to be his favourite thing to do.

Top right: Celebrating twenty-five years of the Children's Film Foundation.

—Battle of Britain—

The Royal Gala for The Battle of Britain was to be held at the Dominion Theatre. They were all called theatres, the big cinemas, and they did have stages, lighting, back-stages, dressing rooms and stage doors, all the facilities for performers and performances. John Thompson told me when he was manager at the Dominion for the year or so before he was promoted to Leicester Square, the film showing there was *The Sound of Music*. Every single house was a sell-out in advance. All the figures except the kiosk and bar sales could be done during the day, knowing that every seat was sold, so in advance of the evening house, he could easily take an hour off, and he did – relaxing in a warm bath in the glamorous star number one dressing room!

But back to The Battle of Britain! While there were to be simultaneous premieres all over Britain – in Belfast, Birmingham, Cardiff, Edinburgh, Glasgow, Leeds, Liverpool, Manchester, Newcastle-on-Tyne, Nottingham and Sheffield, the Royal Gala took place at the

Dominion Theatre, Tottenham Court Road, London, at 8.30 p.m. on Monday September 15, 1969. It was to be a very special charity evening, with proceeds donated to the RAF Benevolent Fund and the RAF Association.

Below: The Battle of Britain Dominion Theatre, September 1969.

HM The Queen, the Duchess of Kent, The Duke of Kent, HRHs Prince Charles and Princess Anne.

Because so many members of the Royal family were coming, and the Dominion is a big theatre seating nearly three thousand people, the other West End Managers were drafted in to help.

Also attending this glittering Royal occasion were the Right Honourable the Lord Mayor of London, Sir Charles Trinder, and Lady Trinder, and three hundred and fifty members of the Battle of Britain Fighter Association from Britain, and from Canada, Jamaica, Kenya, Saudi Arabia and New Zealand. Chief of the Air Staff, Air Chief Marshal Sir John Grandy was present, as well as Chief of the Defence Staff and Marshal of the RAF, Sir Charles Elworthy, and of course Lord Hugh Dowding, the man who in 1940 had led 'The Few' to victory.

Many of the film's stars were also present, as well as some of the original combatants who had acted as technical advisors on the production. To add to the supreme sense of occasion, the Central Band of the RAF, augmented by the Fanfare Trumpeters, played before and after the film.

I was really proud to be there. I could remember standing next to my father on a Sydney beach as he and others gathered excitedly around the Royal Airforce war hero Douglas Bader to say thank you. Now here I was at *The Battle of Britain* film premiere celebrating what the RAF had

achieved in the summer and autumn of 1940, on my usual bouquet duty and encouraging people to go through to their seats. As usual there was closed circuit TV for people to watch inside. All the same, it was hard to keep any crowd moving. People were always very keen to spot the stars and there were plenty there that night. And plenty of Royals. The Queen was there of course, and Prince Charles and Princess Anne, and the Duchess of Gloucester, the Duke and Duchess of Kent, Princess Alexandra, and Prince Michael and Princess Michael of Kent. And they were all due to go round the

stepped back to the line-up herself to have more conversation with producer Harry Saltzman. Another glance back. Still not much progress. Prince Charles looked concerned. Further back, the animated line-up conversations continued. There was a slight tap of the royal foot. The Queen smiled at Princess Anne. The Princess looked back along the line. The Duchess of Gloucester noticed and quickened her pace. Behind her however, things were still very slow.

One of the Queen's staff leaned in to hear what she wanted. 'Go and tell them to hurry up,' she said very firmly. The gentleman disappeared down behind the line. Aware she'd been overheard, the Queen gave a quick high laugh, and smiled all round. The Duchess of Gloucester stepped forward to join Princess Anne and Prince Charles. Down the line things improved – a little. The Queen glanced across at the entrance door and back along the line. Her staff member drew close again. 'Tell them I'm going in,' she said. He set off. Seconds later she turned. The signal button was pressed. The Queen, followed by Prince Charles, Princess Anne, and the Duchess of Gloucester swept in. The fanfare began.

In the foyer there was royal panic. The slow ones gathered quickly beside the entrance, but for them things were already out of hand. The National Anthem began. They had to stand to attention. Once that was over, they hurried

line-up of stars. The Queen set off at her usual businesslike pace, but immediately after her, Prince Charles began to slow things up. Princess Anne was next, but was managing to keep close behind her brother. Next came the Duchess of Gloucester, while the others, including Princess Michael of Kent, Princess Alexandra, and the Duchess of Kent, renowned for their long friendly exchanges with guests, were really lagging behind.

Near the entrance to the circle, at the end of the line, my two youngsters delivered the bouquet to the Queen. All very neat. So far so good.

The Queen glanced back along the line, then she

inside, with all the difficulties of reaching and settling into their seats in the dark, and with the overture to the stage show already under way. I never saw that slowness happen again, but then of course there was never such a gathering of Royals at one premiere again either. *The Battle of Britain* had brought them all together. No film title that followed over the next few years could possibly command such royal patronage. And as one film critic of the day put it: "There will never be another aviation film quite like it."

—Love if There's Time—

n December 1969 came the opening night of *On Her Majesty's Secret Service* with the Marlboro cigarette man, George Lazenby as the new Bond – a Bond that might actually find a woman he might stay with. But of course the story doesn't work out that way! You can't have James Bond settling down! Nor did George Lazenby settle into the role. On this opening night he arrived late and worse for wear, and seemed to me to be crossing swords with producer Cubby Broccoli in the circle foyer. John overheard Broccoli say GL would never work again in Hollywood. I wondered at the time myself – and indeed Lazenby certainly never appeared as Bond again.

Standing on the front of house talking to me didn't seem to be enough for John Thompson now. He began taking me out to lunch sometimes. That was surprising, especially if the theatre was very busy. How did he make the time? We were talking about the theatre, and staffing, but he would sit there smiling across the table at me.

I was warned by the Senior Assistant Manager that Mr Thompson was married. That astonished me since he was always at the theatre, day and night. He never seemed to be away from it for a second. It was also true it wasn't me making eyes at him. It was him always standing talking to me. I would be taking tickets at the doors to the auditorium, or dealing with an incoming queue, or in some other place where I didn't have the choice of moving away. Even though I managed to find a way to mention to him about him being married, nothing altered. Indeed he increased the time he spent talking to me. 'I've booked a weekend in Paris,' he said one day. 'Separate rooms.'

Decimalisation was coming. The money that staff handled every day with sales was due to change in February 1971, and so a good year in advance of it, I was sent on a Rank Organisation training course to be able to train the staff, and two new Assistant Managers as well. We would all need time to learn about how to deal with the new values and coins. I was busy too making myself a special dress in maroon silk for the 1970 Royal Film Performance of *Anne of a Thousand Days* which was coming to the Odeon that February. I wanted to create something with a Tudor panel to celebrate the historical context of the film.

Far left: Premiere, December 1969, On Her Majesty's Secret Service.
Right: George Lazenby with his wife Christina Gannett.
Overleaf: The Premiere of Marooned, January 1970.
Gregory Peck and Ava Gardner.
Harry Secombe.
Roger Moore.
Danny La Rue.
Goldie Hawn.
Stirling Moss.
Dustin Hoffman.
Dame Edith Evans.
RH James Callaghan and Mrs Callaghan.

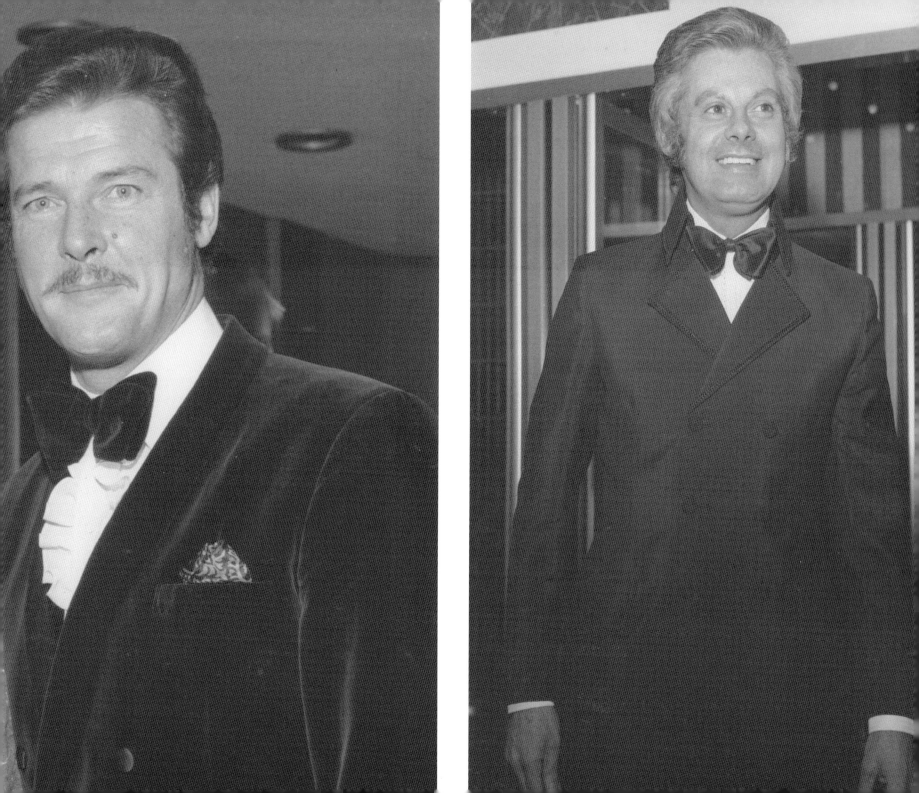

As it turned out, I wore the dress in the January at the premiere of *Marooned!* Gregory Peck, Ava Gardner, Goldie Hawn, Roger Moore, Stirling Moss... there were lots of world-famous high flyers there. The first ever Jumbo Jet in the world had taken off six days before the premiere, and this film was about three astronauts trapped in space. And now I was about to travel myself!

My work visa was due to expire and I sent in my Australian passport as usual to the Home Office to extend my stay. I received it back immediately saying my time in the UK was over! John was appalled. The Rank Organisation was shocked and wrote to the Home Office on my behalf. But no! I had ten days to leave the country! I went back and forth to the Home Office, Australia House, and back again to the Home Office. I had a sister married to the British actor Paul Daneman, and living in London, and a great grandfather, two grandfathers, and a grandmother who were all British, but that was of no help. It was eventually suggested the Rank Organisation might want to apply for a work permit for me, but I couldn't possibly be allowed to be in the country while they did so! The only thing to do was to leave, and there was absolutely no certainty I could return. I decided

the only solution was to go home to my family in Australia and see what might happen.

Back in Adelaide I watched the Royal Film Performance of *Anne of a Thousand Days* on television! John wrote to me all the time, even saying he would come out to Australia himself, if I couldn't return. I was amazed!

Then the miracle happened. As I had been trained in Cinema management in Rank's flagship, and in staff training for decimalisation, I was granted an unconditional

Employment Voucher and I could return immediately. I flew into Heathrow just after the premiere of Airport in April. While I had been away John had made arrangements for his family to move to the coast. He had decided I was moving in with him. Actually I had anticipated sharing a flat with a friend of mine, but when John picked me up at the airport, I found out we were both going to share the flat with her to begin with, but he had in mind a proper move for us, somewhere we would be together. It was an extraordinary

The Royal Film Performance from twelve thousand miles away.

very kind driver from a Black Cab jumped out of his taxi to help. He managed to ram the gear-stick into first gear, and I drove along Piccadilly, around Hyde Park Corner, through Knightsbridge and Hammersmith and all the way home to Chiswick in that gear!

Every day I parked in the tiny private chained-off car park behind the Leicester Square Theatre, or in the Odeon alleyway. The only trouble with the alleyway was that sometimes people parked in the Square across the entrance into it, or across the Charing Cross Road entrance, so when the theatres had closed for the night and we emerged around 11.30 p.m. it could be impossible to get our Mini out!

Never mind! John had a wonderful arrangement with what was then the Garrick Restaurant in Irving Street. If we were stuck, we walked down there, and at a downstairs

A new life begins: John and Felicity in London.

moment. I was back in London, back in Leicester Square, John and I moved in together, and life was completely altered.

We bought a little old red Mini which I drove in and out from Chiswick where we settled. There were no restrictions then, so I drove in Oxford Street, Piccadilly, Mayfair, in fact anywhere in the West End. There was one moment when I was heading out of Panton Street into Haymarket to go home early from the theatre, about 6 o'clock, peak hour, when the Mini's gear stick gave up! I couldn't get it out of neutral, and I was holding up all the West End traffic! A

table, the delightful restaurant owner would bring out the juicy bones of the beef he had carved and served from that evening. The meat still left on them was delicious – a wonderful way of having a late-night supper! And John could have a whisky, because I would be driving home! By the time we came out, the cars blocking us in at one end or the other of the alley had gone and we could escape!

The working days were long ones. The theatre Box Office opened at 10 a.m. and the management came in then too for operational work, and usually the first showing of the current film at the Odeon began at 1.30 p.m. The next showing started at 4 p.m. the next at 6.30 p.m. then the last one at 8 p.m. There was a wonderful question people would ask on the front of house. 'What time is the eight o'clock performance?' That always made me laugh! And of course, performances ran about twenty minutes later over the road in the Leicester Square Theatre, so there was time to nip over the road to help see that house in so that there were two managers, one in the office available if necessary, and the other on front of house duty. Then it was back to the Odeon for an intermission if necessary or to see the next house in. Back and forth, back and forth! On Saturdays in both the Odeon and the LST there were the late-night shows of the films starting around 11 p.m., with both theatres finally closing by 1.45 a.m. and taxis home provided for the staff.

Top right: Premiere of The Secret of Santa Vittoria, June 1970.
Bottom right: Princess Alexandra and Anthony Quinn.

64

—Dangerous Days—

The *Secret of Santa Vittoria*, starring Anthony Quinn and Anna Magnani, was our next important premiere at the Odeon, with Princess Alexandra as the Royal guest. That June in 1970 Edward Heath was elected as Prime Minister. There was trouble in Ireland, and a Dockers' strike in July.

On July 16th the Ken Hughes film *Cromwell* premiered at the Odeon and set a new first week box office record. The Duchess of Gloucester was the Royal guest on the opening night. It must have been a tough choice for the Royals to know who to send. Cromwell harks back to Charles I and that King's battles with Parliament, and his ultimate execution. His grandfather Henry VIII had broken the country away from Rome. The new Anglican Church comprised the Church of England and the Church of Ireland – and then there was still the Catholic Church. When Henry VIII's daughter Queen Elizabeth I came to the throne, she was Supreme Governor of the Church of England. Her successor James I, the son of Elizabeth's cousin, the Catholic Mary Queen of Scots, inherited the English Protestant throne – and then his son Charles inherited it from him. Though Charles I was a fervent Anglican, he married a devout Catholic. He insisted on maintaining his lavish royal lifestyle and fighting expensive and unsuccessful battles, and when Parliament didn't agree with him, he dissolved it. His loyalty to his Catholic wife and deep belief in his own divine right to rule, and Cromwell's religious fervour and common man anti-monarchy ideas didn't mix.

In the film Alec Guinness plays Charles I and Richard Harris is the Puritanical Cromwell. 'Has this King forgotten the Reformation?' Cromwell shouts, throwing the Royal Mace to the House of Commons floor. 'Is the Catholic Church to have a seat in this Parliament?'

Two years earlier in 1968 there had been two days of street battles in Londonderry. At the beginning of 1969 there were clashes in Ulster, and in this spring of 1970, there were snipers in the Belfast streets. Then Ulster Catholics cheered British troops into the city and watched as a 'peace wall' was erected. But soon firebombs were being thrown and Bernadette Devlin was arrested. For the new Ulster party, Gerry Fitt was trying to speed reforms.

With *Cromwell* on now at the Odeon, we had to be more aware of public safety and Bow Street police officers came to give us advice. We were already doing security checks every day before we opened, and before we closed the doors at night – inspecting every row of seats to make absolutely sure nothing was out of place. All exits were thoroughly checked and locked. Because we had a night cleaning staff, they were briefed to watch out for anything unusual. We held rehearsals. We already had fire drill before we opened every Sunday about how to clear the theatre. Now the staff had to understand the added dangers and what was expected of them. Over the next couple of years as trouble in Ireland and on the mainland increased, our security tightened as bomb warnings were rung through direct to premises. With police information about what to expect, and what might be real, if I was the Duty Manager, I was individually responsible for the hour-to-hour safety of the cinema-goers and staff in the theatre. In the Odeon, that could be two thousand people, or fourteen hundred in the LST.

One of the most difficult and on-going examples of sole responsibility were hoax telephone calls. If a warning was given, and as time went on it became almost usual to get three or four a week, the caller would be transferred to the old-fashioned extension phone beside the switchboard operator. Because a great deal of management time was spent in the downstairs foyer 'seeing the house in' and being available to deal immediately with any queries or concerns, it meant that one spent time in the area just near the main switchboard by the main booking office, and the downstairs cloakroom. Sometimes company or customer calls came

Above: Premiere of Cromwell July 1970.
Right: The Duchess of Gloucester receives her bouquet.
Far right: Frank Finlay looks on as Richard Harris is introduced to the Duchess of Gloucester.

through that needed to be dealt with, and it was not unusual to be summoned through to that phone. The warning calls came through like that too, with the telephonist signalling nervously across the cloakroom counter for attention.

The caller would always want to speak to the manager. If the call was an authentic warning, the caller would give a code number, and then say something like 'you have ten minutes to clear the theatre'. It might be fifteen minutes if you were lucky! But if you heard a code number (and they were known and provided to us by Scotland Yard or Bow Street and often changed) you knew the call was genuine.

So, there were just minutes to instruct the projectionist to stop the film, bring up the house lights, and sound a warning bell! And for you, the manager, to announce over the sound system that people must quickly and calmly leave the theatre by the nearest exit! And next, announcing again – with, or loudly without, a megaphone, from the stage at the Odeon, or from the front stalls in the LST, please to keep calm and leave the theatre as quickly as possible – and instructing the staff to check the toilets quickly, assist any members of the public who needed help, then to leave the theatre themselves and gather outside at the prearranged area. Then as manager, make sure that had all happened, and finally to leave yourself!

But there was a darker side to the problem too. While the dangers were real, there were also hoax calls, calls that did not provide a code. Were they real? Might the caller be genuine and have forgotten to include the code through nervousness about what he was doing? There was a dreadful choice to make. If one cleared the theatre at every unsubstantiated call, then the number of hoaxes could increase. If one didn't and the call was real … well, it didn't bear thinking about.

And there was one particular caller who was a real challenge. A call would come through. I would be passed the phone as usual, and I would be told a bomb had been placed inside the theatre, but with no code number given. But if I stepped sideways and looked through the front of house doors up to the red telephone box at the top of the Square, I could see someone in there on the phone, looking down towards the Odeon doors. As soon as I hung up, the person in the phone box did too. He would step out and stand looking down towards the theatre, as if waiting to see what would happen. And I had the awful choice to make. Did I believe him – or whoever it was calling? It was always a fearful moment of decision, whether it was him, and whether one day he might be being serious. For weeks he rang about three times a week, and that person would be in the red phone box, hang up when I did, and emerge and stare down at the theatre...

There was one occasion when I did have to clear the theatre. Right code, legitimate warning. It was scary, but because we did practise, it went smoothly. Public announcement. Me with the megaphone on stage. All the correct procedures. And fire brigades, ambulances, police cars – they all arrived! Immediately afterwards, Bow Street police searched the theatre. Nothing was found. It had been done to cause trouble, but on that occasion, there was no question. The theatre was cleared.

It was an extraordinary time. Remember, with a popular film, one might have two thousand people inside the Odeon, two thousand people in the queue, and another two thousand people milling about outside in the Square. And even more waiting to go into the LST, queuing over there, down St Martin's Street, and milling around on that south side of the Square.

Films came and went. In that August in 1970 Carlo Ponti's film *Sunflower* starring Sophia Loren and Marcello Mastroianni opened in the LST. Then Robert Aldridge's film *Too Late the Hero*, starring Michael Caine and Cliff Robertson, came to the Odeon next, a film about the war against the Japanese in the Pacific.

Below: Tora Tora Tora opens at the Leicester Square Theatre, October 1970.
Top right: The Japanese Ambassador and his wife.
Below middle right: Ernie Wise.
Below far right: Tony Curtis.

It was followed in October by the film *Tora Tora Tora* about the surprise Japanese air strike on Pearl Harbour that brought the Americans into WW2. The Japanese Ambassador in London attended the premiere at the Leicester Square Theatre. Photos show Roy Money, the manager I knew so well from Odeon Haymarket, but now at the Odeon Marble Arch, there to help on the premiere night. What a difficult evening it must have been for him. During the war he had been a prisoner of war working on the fearful Burma Thailand railway.

The Japanese pilot who led the raid on Pearl Harbour, Mitsuo Fuchida, who after the war had become a Presbyterian Minister, was there too and can still be seen on YouTube footage of the *Tora Tora Tora* premiere. When the Pearl Harbour attack took place on 7th December 1941, Winston Churchill said he went to bed and slept the sleep of the saved that night. *Tora Tora Tora* won an Academy Award for Best Special Effects, and huge acclaim in Japan.

In between those two films came *Waterloo* at the Odeon with a wonderful cast: Rod Steiger as Bonaparte, Christopher Plummer as the Duke of Wellington, Orson Welles as Louis XVIII, and Jack Hawkins as General Thomas Picton. The film, which was acclaimed for its lavish battle scenes, was unusually a co-production between the Soviet Union and Italy, and filmed in the Ukraine.

The *Private Life of Sherlock Holmes* followed in December. Meanwhile the important thing was to investigate and get the staff familiar with the new decimal coinage and notes. Day after day we played selling games in the staff room and the

Above: Waterloo, October 1970, attended by HM The Quee
Below: Christopher Plummer; Rod Steiger.

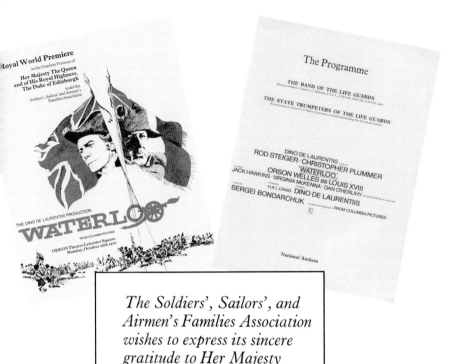

Above: Premiere, The Private Life of Sherlock Holmes
December 1970.
Below: Princess Alexandra receives her bouquet.

The Soldiers', Sailors', and Airmen's Families Association wishes to express its sincere gratitude to Her Majesty The Queen and to His Royal Highness The Duke of Edinburgh for graciously attending tonight's Premiere.

Royal Retiring Room, writing out cheques, giving change for kiosk purchases and ice-creams, thinking what things were worth and what the new coins were called, and working out what the new money looked and felt like.

1971 – Decimalisation arrived on 15th February just after the film *Murphy's War* starring Peter O'Toole had opened. The currency change went very smoothly for us and John was pleased. The public had slight moments of confusion, but the staff felt confident because they had practised and practised handling the new currency.

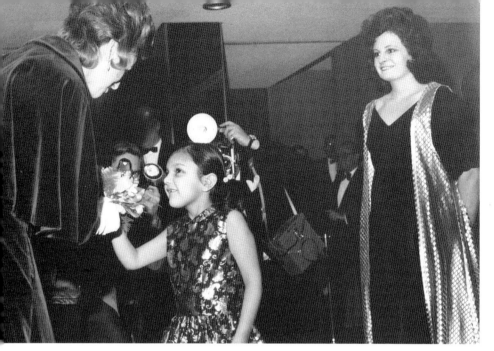

A gentle push at the right moment is part of her job

Royal film performances and *premieres* are routine for an attractive young Australian, Felicity Kinmont, who is one of the assistant managers at the two Rank cinemas in Leicester Square—the Odeon and the Leicester Square Theatre.

Next Royal Film Performance at the Odeon will be on March 8 when Queen Elizabeth the Queen Mother will see the American film, "Love Story".

One of Miss Kinmont's responsibilities on these occasions is the small child chosen to present the traditional bouquet of flowers to the Royal guest. This involves reassuring the child, if she or he is nervous, seeing that the child does not wander off beforehand and giving a gentle push at the psychological moment so that the child arrives at the right spot at the right time to present the flowers. And if there are several members of the Royal Family present this could mean several bouquet-bearing children to keep an eye on.

As Felicity Kinmont is always hovering in the background she feels some members of the Royal Family think she is the mother of an enormous family.

As there is an annual Royal Film Performance at the Odeon and about six Royal Film *Premieres* a year, she has seen most of the Royal Family since she joined the theatre staff in December, 1967.

She was made an assistant manager in 1968, and is believed to be the first woman to hold such a position in a West End cinema.

"A few women have now invaded this male stronghold in the West End," she says. "Of course, I am not the first woman manager appointed by Rank. The company has several women managing theatres around Britain."

Tasmanian born Felicity lived in Sydney, where she trained as a ballet dancer, before coming to London in 1965.

She has appeared as a dancer in pantomime in the Midlands, at a night club in Germany and at a holiday camp on the east coast near Lowestoft.

Felicity's elder sister, Meredith, is married to actor Paul Daneman.

In Leicester Square it was always a world of business – big business. To add to the best British and Hollywood films, within a couple of years we were showing Chinese films and Indian films late at night, and midnight football matches from Italy. And now, in the middle of the night, Boxing matches were going to be beamed in, via satellite as they happened in America.

The Royal Film Performance in March 1971 was *Love Story* with the Queen Mother and Princess Margaret coming. There's still film of them arriving on YouTube. With big royal events, there was a rota with the management as to who would come in early at 7 a.m. On this occasion it fell to me. The theatre needed a thorough safety inspection by the Bow Street police and their dogs, the bouquets would arrive to be put in the Ice-room refrigerator, the contractors putting the Royal box in the front circle needed a cup of tea and some friendly banter, the florists needed to start work to decorate the royal box and the kiosk, and the cleaners needed encouragement and praise for their hard work to make the theatre sparkling. Starting so early was going to make it a long day!

Love Story was an emotional film starring Ali MacGraw, and even the Queen Mother emerged from the film with tears in her eyes. It was an unusual moment for the staff all lined up at the bottom of the staircase. The royal car was late – really unusual, but the Queen Mother rose to the occasion beautifully, using the few minutes to go along the line of staff talking to each person. They were all absolutely thrilled and applauded her as she and Princess Margaret left. But now we were going to be really busy.

That night the Queen Mother was giving ground to Muhammed Ali!

Far left: The bouquet moment – Princess Alexandra.
Below: Love Story, The Royal Film Performance, March 1971.

PROGRAMME

ALYN AINSWORTH AND HIS ORCHESTRA

CLOSED CIRCUIT TELEVISION
Presented by THAMES TELEVISION LTD.

Produced by JIM POPLE   Interviews by MICHAEL PARKINSON
With GERALD SHAW at the Console of the Odeon Theatre Organ

THE STATE TRUMPETERS OF THE LIFE GUARDS
By Permission of Colonel I. B. Baillie
(Lt.-Col. Commanding Household Cavalry)
Director of Music: Capt. A. J. Richards, F.T.C.L., p.s.m.

"KING GEORGE V"
Data Film Distributors present a short film on the life of the
famous steam locomotive.

STAR STAGE PRESENTATION
"PREFACE"

Arranged and Produced by
VIVIAN A. COX

Assisted by
SHIRLEY GAZE
with
THE YOUNG GENERATION

Heather Beckers	Carolyn Heywood	Bobby Bannerman	Rhys Nelsen
Marie Betts	Linda Jolliff	Chris Cooper	Jeremy Robinson
Ann Chapman	Kay Korda	Roger Finch	Brian Rogers
Jackie Dalton	Linda Lawrence	Richard Gough	Kenneth Warwick
Denise Fone	Sandy Penson	Harry Higham	Trevor Willis
Carole Forbes	Susan Toogood	Roger Howlett	Roger Hannah
Lynda Herbert	Wei Wei Wong	Nigel Lythgoe	Michael Howe
	Lara Shawe	Chris Hennen	

Choreographed and Staged by **DOUGLAS SQUIRES**
Vocal Direction and Musical Arrangements by **ALYN AINSWORTH**
Costumes: **DORINDA CUTTING**
Lighting: **DICKIE HIGHAM**

The Young Generation are produced and directed by **STEWART MORRIS**.

Top left: John Mills and his wife
Mary Hayley Bell.
Above: Shirley Bassey.
Left: Dora Bryan.

Left: Tony Curtis.
Below: Oscar Bernstein presents Olivier De Havilland and Ray Milland to the Queen Mother.
Right: Bouquet moments; a Royal smile for John.

—From Royals to the Boxing Ring—

As soon as the Queen Mother and Princess Margaret were gone, and the theatre audience had cleared, the red carpet was rolled up. The huge flower display was swept off the kiosk in the downstairs foyer, the royal box in the front circle was dismantled by the contractors, and all the exits were closed and checked. During the evening I had set up a bar for VIPs on the main office desk in the upstairs managers' office – white linen cloth, champagne, scotch, martinis and more, and we had carried stock to the downstairs and upstairs cloakrooms, so as well as the licensed bar, extra drinks bars could be set up in those. It was a very different audience we would be opening the doors to at 1 a.m.

Beamed in from Madison Square Garden in America via satellite and showing on the Odeon screen: Muhammed Ali v Joe Frazier! The fight of the century! It was to be an exciting night – a match between two undefeated fighters, each with a legitimate claim to be World Heavyweight Champion.

From midnight, crowds were banging on the front of house doors! How different from the Royal Film Performance crowd the Boxing fraternity was! Nearly all men! Big thick cigars! You could still smoke in cinemas then, though once inside the auditorium, only in the back circle. Nearly all of the men were dressed in beautiful and expensive looking camel coats!

When we opened at 1 a.m., checking the tickets was quite a task. Just two of the main doors were opened. The rest were kept closed with staff on the inside to make sure those doors stayed closed. We had several attempts of young men and youngsters trying to storm the open doors! One boy managed to break through, and disappear, but I had seen his face, and I scoured the crowds until I found him. We cheerfully agreed between us he didn't have a ticket, and I put him out one of the side ground-floor exits, though that made me realise we should be staffing those doors more effectively. If one person got in and thought of it, they could let in all their friends that way. John sent two members of staff to each one. Things began to calm down a little. The initial rush was over. People were coming in more sensibly.

I was asked to take some of the special guests upstairs to the office VIP bar. The windows were open for air because the office door was very carefully closed with a member of staff on the outside. I was pouring champagne when suddenly a young boy of about fifteen fell through the open window, landing straight into the centre of the desk bar! Bottles crashed over! Glasses fell! There was champagne everywhere! The boy was as surprised as we were! He immediately jumped to the floor looking for a way out, and a couple of the VIP guests grabbed him. We were all laughing with shock and he was cheerfully escorted down the stairs and out the side exit! It turned out he had climbed to the first floor up the drainpipe in the alley! It was a complete miracle he hadn't fallen. One of the theatre handymen was sent immediately to put some grease on the drainpipe to deter any other adventurous break-ins!

Once that private office bar was back up and running, I went to the downstairs kiosk to help Ralph, the excellent confectionary sales manager, cook hot dogs! That certainly

36 Golden Square London W1R 4AH. Telephone 01-734 8080

9th March 1971

Dear Mr Thompson

I would like to thank you for your magnificent organisation last night. It was so helpful in making the show such a great success, and made my job very much easier.

Once again, many thanks.

Yours sincerely,

Cecil G. Bernstein

Cecil G Bernstein

John Thompson Esq
The Manager
Odeon Cinema
Leicester Square
London W 1

11/BJM/GS

Royal Film Performance 1971

R.F.P. COMMITTEE

CECIL G. BERNSTEIN,
President, The Cinema and
Television Benevolent Fund

RALPH S. BROMHEAD, F.C.A.

KENNETH RIVE
President, Cinematograph
Exhibitors' Association

MRS. GWYNETH DUNWOODY
Director, Film Production Association
of Great Britain

MONTAGUE C. MORTON
President, Kinematograph
Renters' Society Ltd.

PETER KING
Managing Director
EMI Cinemas & Leisure Ltd.

BRYAN QUILTER
Managing Director,
Rank Leisure Services Ltd.

THEO COWAN
Film Publicity Guild

SIR GEOFFREY COX, C.B.E.
Chairman of the Independent
Television Companies Association

★

Executive Director:
MAJOR-GENERAL
C. M. GRIGG, C.B.E., M.C.

Secretary:
C. A. A. KILMISTER

TELEPHONES:
01-437 6567 (3 lines)

★

Advertisement Director:
STANLEY C. MILLS
Telephone: 01-629 5991 or 9141

IN THE GRACIOUS PRESENCE OF
HER MAJESTY QUEEN ELIZABETH THE QUEEN MOTHER

at the Odeon Theatre, Leicester Square, London, W.C.2
Monday, 8th March, 1971
to Aid the Cinema and Television Benevolent Fund

ROYALTY HOUSE, 72 DEAN STREET, LONDON, W.1., W1V 6LT
CAAK/HIW   9th March, 1971

John Thompson, Esq.,
Odeon Theatre,
Leicester Square,
London, W.C.2.

Dear John,

Although feeling rather tired but happy this morning, we can only look back on last night's Royal Film Performance with satisfaction and pleasure.

It must have been a long and weary night for you, what with the Boxing and so on but I do want you to know how very much we appreciate all that you did to make the evening go so well and so successfully.

We really are very grateful to you indeed and perhaps you would be kind enough to convey our thanks also to all those members of your staff who worked so well with you.

It was a great evening and of enormous value to the Fund.

Thank you again and all best wishes,

Yours sincerely,

Tony

C.A.A. Kilmister,
Secretary

TELEGRAMS & CABLES : CINBENFUND LONDON W.I

Left: Cecil Bernstein sends his congratulations.
Above: Congratulations from the Secretary of the Royal
Film Performance Committee.

wasn't the usual offering from there, but everything was specially set up to cater for this new crowd, and hot dogs proved very popular! Eventually people began to file into the stalls and up the stairs to the circle.

Once the fight began, there were constant cheers and shouts coming from the auditorium. The first rounds were even, but Frazier began to have the advantage. Apparently! I never saw the fight! The theatre was far too busy! People came out between rounds, swallowed down drinks, ordered more hot dogs, and then crowded back into the auditorium again.

Keeping up with the bar stock in three bars was an enormous task. I was up and down the back stairs with crates and crates of beer, and more and more spirits – for hours. At about 4 a.m. I went into the Ladies in the upstairs foyer, and promptly went to sleep on the loo! I was woken by the loudest shouts of the night! Joe Frazier had won, but Ali had fought well, so the crowds went home satisfied that they had been there to see the fight of the century!

The theatre looked like a tornado had hit it! The night cleaners arrived to rescue it. The reception staff fell into taxis home. The extra bars needed unpacking. About 6 a.m. the management finally filed downstairs into the Royal Retiring Room where we had a well-deserved glass or two of leftover champagne! For the rest of the new day, we wandered around dazed. The film *When Eight Bells Toll* starring Anthony Hopkins, Jack Hawkins and Robert Morley opened that day on continuous performance. That meant you could buy a ticket at any time, and go in during the film, provided there were seats, and stay through to that point in the next showing. If you did do that, it was like seeing

the middle and end before the beginning! For me that day felt a bit that way anyway! With the long day and night I'd already had, I certainly couldn't have thought which was the beginning, middle or end of any part of this new day! When John and I finally went home to bed, we both slept soundly for twelve hours! And thankfully we had the next day off!

—Decisions Matter—

Sometimes we had films that didn't take much money. That April in 1971 in the LST, the film *Last Valley* took just £800 on its first day. Luckily business picked up the next day to £2,200! But takings fell away again the following week. But there was always something going on.

As Duty Manager on any evening, I had to count in the money from the kiosk and the bars, and add those figures to the figures received from the box office which specified the cash, cheques, advance bookings and agency bookings listed onto the huge accounting sheet – about 60 cm by 40 cm, and the other takings had to be added to that. And it all had to balance across and down! And then of course the bar, ice-room and kiosk cash had to be taken across the Square to the Bank's Night Safe.

In the daytime, checking the stock against 'take' in the bars was one of my weekly jobs. I invented a set of rulers with markings to show how many measures of scotch or gin, or martinis, or other drinks were still in each bottle, and so how much had been used. For instance, there were thirty-one measures of spirits to a standard bottle, so with my carefully marked rulers, I could be quite accurate. Sherry, Martini, Wine – remember those popular wines like Blue Nun, Niersteiner and Liebfraumilch? Everything could be gauged and weekly bar takings calculated from that. It certainly improved the operation of the bar in the Odeon, and across the road at the LST as well. And now, apart from the Reception staff, I began training young Assistant Managers not only for Leicester Square but for Rank's other West End theatres too.

1971 was an eventful year. Astronauts drove on the moon in July. In August riots flared in Ulster and all processions were cancelled, but at the same time the new and exciting Ulster International Motorcycle Grand Prix began too. The IRA threatened to start bombing the mainland, and the Post Office tower was blasted by a bomb on October 31st – on its observation platform. Now we really had to be very, very careful.

I remember one day when I was on duty in the Leicester Square Theatre, a lady came hurrying towards me in the foyer. 'Someone has left a briefcase in the stalls,' she told me urgently. I followed her down the stairs. Inside the auditorium there were people out in both aisles, standing well away from a row about halfway down. She pointed to the centre where there was indeed a briefcase on the seat. 'A man came in with it, chose a seat, and then went out, leaving the briefcase there.'

Given the difficulties at the time, leaving a bag unattended was the last thing to do, even if the man had just taken himself to the toilet. I glanced around. The agitation was obvious, and there was no sign of the man coming back. 'Did he say to anyone where he was going?' That would have been quite common practice then. Everyone shook their heads. It was a suitcase kind of business bag, but left in full sight. If someone wanted to plant trouble, they would be more likely to put it under the seat. I looked around. Everyone watching took another step back.

It would be difficult to clear the theatre. I would have to do it without a megaphone, against music, and without time to advise the staff, or the projection box. There had been no warning call. I made a quick and daring decision. I went into the row and examined the appearance of the briefcase. Ordinary, but then it would be! I touched it lightly. Nothing happened. I picked it up gingerly. Nothing happened. I moved slowly and carefully out of the row, and up the aisle. People backed away, staring at me. Emerging into the downstairs foyer, I made for the cloakroom on the far side, which ran down and deep under narrow little St Martins Street at the side of the theatre. I took the key from the girl on duty and told her to go out and across to the staircase. I placed the bag down very, very carefully at the back of the area where the many coats hanging up might muffle a blast, and came out, locking the door behind me.

I mustered staff and put them on duty near the staircase so no-one had access to any part of the downstairs foyer. I went upstairs to the box office and halted ticket sales while I asked the staff in there to phone Bow Street so I could get advice.

A moment later there was a man beside me. 'What,' he was shouting, 'have you done with my briefcase?' I breathed a sigh of relief. If he was dangerous, he wouldn't be here shouting, drawing attention to himself. I explained in no uncertain terms that given the dangers of leaving any items unattended in a public place, the bag had been removed. Did he realise how many people he had frightened? Did he realise the police could be involved? 'I went out into the Square to make a phone call. Give me back my briefcase, and I'll go and watch the film.' I didn't think he deserved that! Nor did I believe the people around him would be happy to see him come back into the auditorium. I agreed to return the briefcase, but also to use my right as Theatre Manager to deny him access to the cinema, and given the nuisance he had caused, definitely not to return his money. He was pretty cross when I made him wait outside with a member of staff, while I went down for the briefcase. I wasn't afraid of it now. The man had just been really silly, and not for one moment thought about the disturbance and public fear he could cause. Before the film began, I went back into the auditorium to make sure that the people there knew what had happened, so they could relax and enjoy themselves.

New films came and went all the time. In September *Carnal Knowledge* opened at the Leicester Square Theatre and generated record box office takings of £13,600 in its first week (equivalent of £196,500 in 2020) and £12,000 in its second week. Meanwhile over the Square at the Odeon, Lionel Blair came in early one day to see the stage and dressing rooms to make preparations for a stage show to include Disney songs sung by stars like Barbara Windsor, Charlie Drake and Harry Corbett on the evening of the coming world premiere of *Bedknobs and Broomsticks*, and John Mills was going to introduce Angela Lansbury on stage. At the one stage rehearsal at the beginning of October, I was making coffee for all, and then the following day running a press reception in the Royal Retiring room after the morning press show.

Right: World Premiere Bedknobs and Broomsticks,
October 1971.

WALT DISNEY PRODUCTIONS PRESENTS

Bedknobs and Broomsticks

WORLD CHARITY PREMIERE
ODEON LEICESTER SQUARE THURSDAY OCTOBER 7th
Sponsored by THE VARIETY CLUB OF GT. BRITAIN
to aid the CINEMA AND TELEVISION BENEVOLENT FUND and the VARIETY CLUB HEART FUND

Walt Disney Productions

The world premiere of *Bedknobs and Broomsticks* on 7th October 1971 was a busy day, and advance bookings on tickets broke yet another record. On that day there was lots of activity in the Square. There's still a BBC archive on Twitter of John Noakes on that day in 1971, helping to change the enormous cinema advertising hording, and showing huge searchlights being installed in the Leicester Square Gardens to shine up into the night sky to add glamour to the evening. A life-size model of Angela Lansbury as the witch was hauled up to the theatre roof to fly on ropes over the Square, and the Odeon foyers were filled with suits of armour because they were part of the witch's spells in the film.

An eight track stereophonic sound system played music from the film to the crowds outside, while David Hamilton interviewed the stars on closed circuit television, with a film unit from the BBC recording the event for young TV viewers.

Bedknobs and Broomsticks was a Disney film, with its songs written by the Sherman brothers. Being shown in the 'famed Odeon' as they called it, seemed to be lucky for the brothers. Every one of their films that premiered there was nominated for at least one Oscar – *Chitty Chitty Bang Bang, Bedknobs and Broomsticks*, and later in 1976, *The Slipper and the Rose*.

On 28th October a majority of one hundred and ten MPs in Parliament voted to enter the European Common Market. At the theatres, all our Reception staff had new uniforms – for the girls, purple dress and jacket with a pale pink-mauve trim down the front of the jacket. Still short hems of course! For the men, purple suits with a pink-mauve shirt and purple bow tie. I was now promoted to Senior Assistant Manager. With Agency Advance bookings increasing, a new white desk arrived for the foyer, to replace the old continuous performance booking central ticket box. On a platform, the desk was the centre for information and reception, prominently positioned right in the middle of the entrance foyer.

On November 17th John went in early to work for a special morning showing of *Nicholas and Alexandra* for Sam Speigal, Harry Saltzman, and King Michael of Romania and his family. The film was due to have its World Charity Premiere at the Odeon on 29th of the month. On 22nd November we were advised that the Queen had Chickenpox so would be unlikely to make the Premiere. Meanwhile David Niven and his wife came to watch another morning run-through of the film.

Top left: Charlie Drake.
Top right: Harry Corbett.
Bottom left: Reg Varney.
Bottom right: Stanley Baxter.

Above left: John Mills and wife Mary Hayley Bell.
Above: Angela Lansbury with David Hamilton.
Bottom left: Syd James.
Bottom right: Mickey Mouse.
Top right: World Charity Premiere Nicholas and Alexandra, November 1971.
Furthest right: Princess Anne arrives.
Far right: Cameras galore!

Princess Anne meets Tom Baker, Janet Suzman, and Michael Jayston.

At the premiere of *Nicholas and Alexandra* on November 29th, Princess Anne came, and so did Lord Mountbatten. There was a wonderful line up of all the stars, photographers and TV cameras, and it was a busy evening. The theatre doors finally closed at 11.20 p.m. and we all headed down the Royal Retiring Room for a well earned glass of wine.

Above: New staff uniforms on show.

—Big Business—

Just after Christmas in 1971, at the Odeon it was *Diamonds are Forever* – the Sean Connery come back. Magnetic and utterly handsome, he was Bond. He could light the cigarette, vanquish the villain, wear the tux, and get the girl. And could he draw the crowds! The day before it was about to open there were complaints – people couldn't get through on the phone! And no wonder! Bond was back! James Bond!

Nicholas and Alexandra had transferred to the Leicester Square Theatre and was still doing really well. On the same day as the Bond film opened in the Odeon, over the road, the LST took £2,104.00 – the equivalent in 2020, according to the CPI, of nearly £30,000. And Bond of course broke all box office records! Six thousand, one hundred and twenty-four people came through the doors and we took £4,653 – if one compares that to 2020, it is £66,000. In one day!

The following day the box office takings for Bond increased to £6,300 – well, there was a showing at midday and a late-night show as well! We needed police help to control the crowds out in the Square! John and I got home at 4 a.m.! We were back in next day for the midday showing. There were enormous queues, with people prepared to fight to get in! Police needed again! The day after that Kenneth Moore, John Profumo with his wife Valerie Hobson, and Alfred Marks were all in to see the film. The following week Stirling Moss came – and Reginald Maudling was featured in an article in the Australian *Melbourne Age* about being really lucky to get a ticket because people were prepared to fight the General Manager for them!

A report in the Melbourne Age
The Age – Jan 25th 1972

DIAMONDS ARE FOREVER

REGGIE MAUDLING was lucky enough to penetrate the jammed switchboard of the Leicester Square Odeon a couple of weeks ago. He was luckier still to get a ticket. "We thought we'd make an exception for the Home Secretary," says J. Arthur Rank.

Others have been less fortunate. One thwarted patron has already blackened the eye of Odeon Manager John Thompson. Yet another who couldn't get in, says he has reported him to the Director of Public Prosecutions.

The fuss? What else? James Bond 007 is back with the biggest licence to make a box office killing that has ever hit British cinema. In its first week at the Odeon, the latest Bond epic, *Diamonds Are Forever*, took nearly £35,000 (about $75,000)...

The black eye story was great advertising but there were real pressures with thousands of people wanting to see the film. The article went on to point out just how much money in Australian currency the Bond films had made, and predicted that *Diamonds Are Forever* would turn out to be one of the most successful films of all time, and quoting Albert 'Cubby' Broccoli saying that the Bond films had taken more than $500 million.

Over the road, *Nicholas and Alexandra* was still doing full houses. The following Saturday after a long day with queues at the Odeon, we had a Charity Late Night Show too – a complete sell out! Both theatres were doing capacity business! The staff and management were given a reward of a late-night champagne party in the Royal Retiring Room! But the hard work went on!

At the end of that busy January in 1972, trouble increased

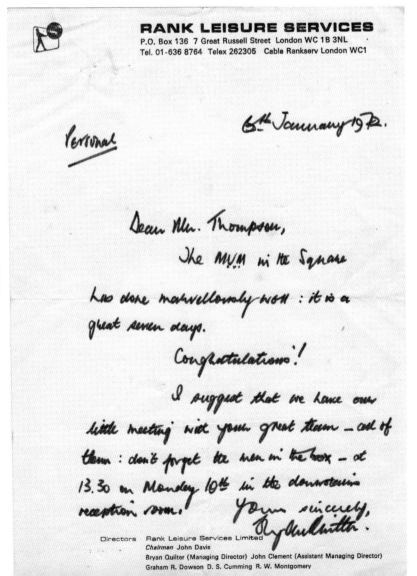

in Ireland when Paratroopers fired on Derry Marchers. The IRA killed British soldiers, and three days later the British Embassy in Dublin was destroyed by fire. Three weeks after that, the Para headquarters in Aldershot was bombed, and a month later a hoax call in Belfast deliberately steered people towards a massive explosion. Within a week Heath imposed direct rule in Ulster. In Leicester Square our safety measures had to be very carefully stepped up, and fast. Meanwhile *Diamonds are Forever* ended its twelve-week run with total box office receipts of £262,484 net, the equivalent in 2020 of nearly three and a half million pounds!

The Royal Film Performance on March 27th was *Mary Queen of Scots*. The Queen Mother was coming, and Princess Margaret. There is still film on YouTube to see of their arrival! British Royalty/Royal Film Premiere/1972.

Shooting film to show inside the auditorium on screen, these cameramen recorded every important occasion – the Royal Film Performances, World and Charity Premieres.

The filming showed Royal arrivals, and the presentations of all the stars and VIPs in the line-up, and the bouquet being presented, finishing as the Royal Fanfare began and the Royal party went in to see the feature film. The audience seated inside could experience the excitement in the crowds, and enjoy everything happening before the actual film – and so could the television viewing public. One end of the circle foyer would be set up too with lights and microphones to speak to the stars – with interviewers like David Frost or Angela Rippon. Before the film started, David Frost was on stage to tell the audience that the evening had raised over £43,000 for the Cinema and Television Benevolent Fund, over half a million pounds today!

Of course, that night at the Royal Film Performance of *Mary Queen of Scots*, the stars and producers of the film were there – and so were other famous people like Keith Michel, Joan Sims, Susan Hampshire, Alan Bates, Susan George, Hildegard Neil, James Mason, Peter Ustinov, and Alan Wicker, and Paul Getty as well. And of course, John would always be in the back of any press picture. He was after all managing everything that was going on!

More films! *Kidnapped* premiered on 4th May. *How to Steal a Diamond* starring Robert Redford and George Segal did well in June, though there were railway strikes affecting the figures. But now in this busy 1972, we had a film coming that would be a Gala World Charity Premiere in both theatres, the Odeon and the Leicester Square Theatre, and all on the same night!

Young Winston, about the early years of Winston Churchill, was directed by Richard Attenborough, and produced by Carl Foreman with a young actor called Simon Ward playing the leading role.

The guest of honour was Baroness Spencer Churchill, with twenty-nine members of her family including Christopher Soames and Nicholas Soames. The Prime Minister Edward Heath, and Labour's Harold Wilson and his wife were there. Noel Coward came, accompanied by the beautiful Marlene Dietrich. There were many other stars too including Rex Harrison, Kenneth More, and even boxing star Henry Cooper.

I was on duty in the Odeon upstairs foyer as the house was going in, and over on one side, Noel Coward was sitting talking to Lady Churchill. She was sitting on the narrow shelf that ran along the edge of the foyer. He was sitting on one of the tall circular ashtrays.

Royal Film Performance 1972 Mary Queen of Scots: Left: Peter Ustinov and James Mason greet the Queen Mother. Above: Five-year-old Rupert Adley presents the bouquet.

Gala World Charity Premiere Young Winston, July 1972.

The young Winstons.

Noel Coward and Marlene Dietrich.

Harold and Mary Wilson.

I was quite fearful that the ashtray wouldn't hold him. It wouldn't hold anyone for very long. I went over and said to him, 'Sir, I don't think that's a very safe seat. Can I get you a proper chair?' I got one for Lady Churchill as well, and then one for Carl Foreman who joined them. I left them sitting there happily deep in more conversation.

Actually this moment brought back a special memory from my childhood – a reception in a very grand hotel in Sydney when my mother took me up with her to collect the winning prize in a national competition for best stage play, judged by Noel Coward. As a successful Australian writer already, my mother Joan Kinmont was absolutely

Left: Noel Coward, Lady Churchill and Carl Foreman.

Right: Christopher Soames, his wife Mary (Churchill) and Prime Minister Edward Heath.

delighted to be presented with her prize by Noel Coward himself, and he patted me on the head! I was about eight or nine years old!

Once the formalities had been carried out in the Odeon, and the film was about to start, Lady Churchill, with the Prime Minister Edward Heath, Churchill family members, several Cabinet members, Richard Attenborough and Carl Foreman, all walked with John across the road to the Leicester Square Theatre, with about eight thousand people out in the Square all cheering Lady Churchill.

With the closed-circuit TV cameras showing it all on both cinema screens, the excitement of the Premiere started all over again! It was a long night making sure everything worked well in both theatres. We saw the house out in the Odeon and then crossed the road to see the LST house out.

We were finally driving home in the Mini at 3 a.m. when we stopped at traffic lights. Richard Attenborough's limousine pulled alongside us. He opened his window and told us how much he had enjoyed the evening and thanked us for all our hard work! The lights changed, and he waved as his chauffeur sped off!

Young Winston took £21,000 in its first week (over £283,000 today), and many interesting people came to see it, including the film star Katherine Hepburn. I remember John rescuing Kenneth Moore from queuing up on a very busy day. In the third week the box office takings were £22,000, and £19,000 in its fourth week. And it went on being busy.

In September, after a busy last day with *Young Winston* before it transferred over the road to the LST the following day, we went on into a late-night satellite showing in the Odeon of a Muhammed Ali v Floyd Patterson fight. Ali won in the eighth round, floating like a butterfly, stinging like a bee! Again it was a long night, and again the theatre was in a bad state afterwards with damaged toilets and smashed windows. We left at 5.45 a.m. The next day, with *Young Winston* opening in the Leicester Square Theatre, we hosted a personal appearance of Simon Ward (Winston) and Richard Attenborough. And over in the Odeon, the new film *Heist* opened.

In November 1972 we had an Advertising Film Festival in the Leicester Square Theatre – a sort of Oscar ceremony for the film ads on television and screen, a very busy daytime event. That month there was another Boxing late night in the Odeon. Muhammed Ali beat Bob Foster this time, again in the 8th round. And again the theatre was left a mess, with people even breaking into the office this time! We showed another fight in January between Ali and Joe Bugnor – Ali won again, but this fight went twelve rounds. More damage, and an even later arrival home – 7 30 a.m.! And that evening there was a Midnight Champagne 'do' in the Odeon for the new film, *Travels With My Aunt.* Never a dull moment!

—Stars and Stripes and Royal Stars—

Because of the recent high takings at the Odeon and Leicester Square Theatres, John had been offered a special kind of bonus by Rank Theatres – two weeks all expenses paid holiday in Los Angeles, courtesy of Columbia Pictures, with Universal Studios and Disney Studios wanting to contribute to the adventure. Lucky me! I was going too! It was an unforgettable experience, a bit like a honeymoon, though John and I weren't married. We stayed in the Beverley Wilshire Hotel – remember that hotel featured in *Pretty Woman*? We were spoilt with luxurious accommodation and a balcony overlooking the city, and beautiful meals every day. We were sent welcoming flowers from Columbia Pictures, and from Ross Hunter, the Producer of their newest film from Columbia Pictures, *Lost Horizon*.

Our glamorous hotel in Hollywood.

Some moments were set aside for our own personal sightseeing, but special days had been arranged to show us the Hollywood dream. We were hosted by the sweetest elderly couple, Matilda and Eli Levy for Columbia Pictures, and were treated to champagne as guests on a yacht in the harbour. We were given a personal guided tour of the city sights: Rodeo Drive, Sunset Boulevard, the Hollywood Hills, and the stars' homes, and I bought a funny little cine-reel of the Los Angeles sights. It was mostly out of focus but it would be fun to take home as a reminder of our travels.

We went to Knott's Berry Farm – a tribute to country and western life and music. At Long Beach we toured the retired ocean liner, which had been turned into a museum, the *Queen Mary*. On one level it was amazingly recreated as a troop ship, complete with radio announcements and wartime sounds, and on the upper decks, there was an elegant show of original steam ship cruising. And down in the hull was an extraordinary aquatic exhibition, the underwater world of ocean explorer Jacques Cousteau.

We entered a world of big screen money and make-believe on our VIP trip around Universal Studios, driven in a private VIP buggy to see all the film sets, attractions and exhibitions. One minute we were nearly swallowed by *Jaws*, and the next we were right in the path of a tidal wave! After lunch with studio executives, we saw haunted houses, man-made waterfalls, Wild West sets, enactments of gun fights with stunt men falling off roof tops, and sets like Alfred Hitchcock's *Psycho* house, and extraordinary countryside and desert illusions. In the evening Columbia Pictures publicity executives treated us to dinner at Jack's-

On-the-Beach where we sat watching the floodlit Pacific Ocean surf rolling in and out over fine white sand.

On one of the days, we were collected in Roy Disney's limousine and driven to Disney Studios where the illustrators were drawing each frame of the forthcoming animation film *Robin Hood*, due to be premiered at the Odeon at the end of the year. Some scenes were complete, while in others, artists were still working on the black and white outlines. It was amazing to see how each subsequent drawing demonstrated just the flick of a whisker, or the slightest turn of the head from the drawing before. The artist could flip through a stack of pages and show how the movement would be on screen. Computer graphics have since offered animators a huge leap forward, but back then each drawing was done by hand, with a model sheet to ensure consistency. Photocopying had speeded up their process. One single drawing could be copied and minutely altered to spread a smile or move a limb. This process was useful too for backgrounds where little changed.

Beside a huge storyboard of the completed scene, one artist was carefully hand colouring a thin film cell in opaque paint. Just a single speck of dust magnified up on screen would ruin it, so every cell was individually checked before being sent to the camera department. The Art Director and Character Designer showed us how the layers for each frame were built up, one behind the other, to give a real sense of depth of field to the finished film, and told us how it was three or four years from the original sketches to a finished production. These days the perfection and mathematical correctness of modern computer animation has added speed and cost effectiveness, but in a way the transition has cost that tremor and tension of an artist's hand, the living breathing quality of an individual's creation. The attention to minute detail remains though, in every leaf flutter, each whisker twitch, making Disney films outstanding, and we could see already that *Robin Hood* would be a huge success when it came to the Odeon in London.

We also saw a magical series of film cuts in very slow motion showing how the early illustrators had developed their ideas of drops of water falling from the forest trees into the pool in the film *Bambi* – how when the drop hit the surface, the surrounding water rose up like a coronet. It was scientific as well as utterly beautiful.

We were treated to a champagne flight to Las Vegas to see the glitzy gambling palaces and to enjoy an evening meal in the desert, before flying back at midnight. We hired a car and drove ourselves down to the Mexican border and looked round an amazing outdoor market, but we could tell how being a just few yards across into Mexico made a huge difference to people's welfare.

Back in Los Angeles when we mentioned we might go briefly to San Francisco, Columbia Pictures immediately booked us into the glamorous downtown Mark Hopkins Hotel for two nights with a view of the Bay to die for! We walked around the colourful Fishermen's Wharf and the shops beside the bay, saw the Golden Gate Bridge, and rode cable cars up and down the steep hills.

But the planned central theme of the fortnight was cinema and everyone was anxious to show us the Hollywood movie dream.

We were collected in a silver limousine at the hotel and driven to the World Premiere of *Lost Horizon*, starring a

Our programme from the Hollywood Premiere of Lost Horizon.

list of wonderful actors including Peter Finch, Liv Ullman, Charles Boyer, and John Gielgud, at the National Theatre, Westwood. We were due to premiere the film for the Royal Film Performance in London just three weeks later, so this was an exciting introduction to what was coming. It was a very dressed up occasion, and we were treated like stars ourselves, and surrounded by famous faces – Dean Martin sitting directly behind us, and Ella Fitzgerald two seats away. The guest list read like a who's who: Luci Arnaz, Jack Benny, Ernest Borgnine, George Burns, Red Buttons, Cyd Charisse, Tony Curtis, Doris Day, Eva Gabor, Mitzi Gaynor, Jerry Lewis, Art Linkletter, Gregory Peck, Rosalind Russell, Dinah Shore, Billy Wilder – and many, many more! Everybody there was famous! After the film we were wined and dined with all these people at the Shangri-la Ball at the Los Angeles Ballroom in the Century Plaza Hotel, sitting at a table with the film's producer Ross Hunter and Columbia Pictures executives!

Our final day was spent at Disneyland. We were guided around every attraction – past hippos rising out of the swamps beside us as we balanced on a tiny river boat; hologram dancers waltzed past as we walked through a Viennese ballroom. We stared up at huge dinosaurs hoping they wouldn't look down; we dodged lions, and hid from huge elephants. We climbed on sailing ships, and poked our fingers through hologram faces that appeared from nowhere, and watched a 'real' Abraham Lincoln give the Gettysburg Address! We travelled to the bubbling centre of the earth, flew to the moon and back on a space ship, and said a personal hello to Mickey Mouse. We were treated to lunch in the VIP restaurant and went on to Sleeping Beauty's castle, and every other attraction we fancied. What a day!

Back in London at the Royal Film Performance of *Lost Horizon*, the Queen looked stunning in a really glittering dress, complemented by a ruby necklace and her diamond tiara. Her arrival, and the 1973 film line-up, is still on YouTube as one of the hits of the Royal Film Performance years. That particular filming also shows photographer Harry Myers who took the fabulous pictures that illustrate this book.

That evening Peter Finch went on stage to give a welcoming speech to the Queen, and to announce that £48,000 had been raised for the CTBF, nearly £600,000 in today's money. There were some wonderful stars attending,

Left: The Mouse!
Above: Lunching with Disney.

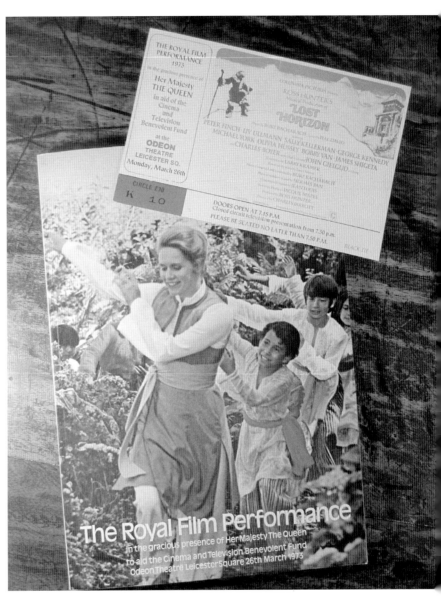

Above left: The Royal Film Performance March 1973,
Lost Horizon.
Left and above: The London Souvenir Programme.

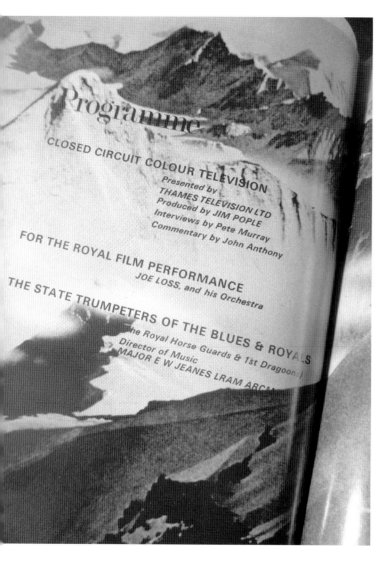

Programme

CLOSED CIRCUIT COLOUR TELEVISION
Presented by
THAMES TELEVISION LTD
Produced by JIM POPLE
Interviews by Pete Murray
Commentary by John Anthony

FOR THE ROYAL FILM PERFORMANCE
JOE LOSS, and his Orchestra

THE STATE TRUMPETERS OF THE BLUES & ROYALS
(The Royal Horse Guards & 1st Dragoons)
Director of Music
MAJOR E W JEANES LRAM ARCM

as well as Ross Hunter and the executives and producers from Columbia Pictures, who had all been so kind to us. Now on this grand occasion we could return some of the hospitality they had shown us in L.A.

At the beginning of May there was a general strike. The theatres were very quiet that day of course. Later that month in America, there was the Watergate crisis. Now at the Odeon there were morning organ concerts. The Duchess, as the theatre's Compton organ was known, and which is still there today, has 1,400 pipes controlled by five keyboards and sits on a rising platform in the middle of the orchestra pit. She came into her own at particular Charity shows. Like the old days in theatre, the organ rose up from the orchestra pit, and the organist then, Gerald Shaw, would play while the house was coming in. He played the National Anthem on premiere nights. His LP 'Fanfare' made the news. He and the Duchess had quite a following, and these morning concerts in the Odeon were always well attended.

Far left: What an evening!
Left: John Thompson greeting the Queen on her arrival.
Right: HM The Queen with Cecil Bernstein.
Overleaf, left: Ross Hunter the film's producer is presented to the Queen.
Overleaf, far right: Felicity's sister photographs her lining up the bouquet presenter.
The bouquet moment.
Such a kind letter from our Columbia Pictures hosts.

COLUMBIA
PICTURES
COLGEMS SQUARE
BURBANK, CALIFORNIA 91505

April 27, 1973

Mr. John Thompson
Manager, Odeon Theatre
Leicester Square WC2
London, England

Dear John:

It was so nice hearing from you and receiving
the photographs of the Premiere, especially
the one with the Queen. "Lost Horizon" is
doing pretty good business in this country.

If you were here now, you would say that you
are in London, because for the last week or so
we have had London weather here. Maybe the
California sunshine went to London.

Mathilda joins me in wishing Felicity and you
all the best in the world and hope you have
"felicity" all your life.

I hope we will have the pleasure of seeing you
again some day. One can never tell, perhaps
here or in London.

All the best.

Sincerely,

Ely Levy

EL:gg

A DIVISION OF COLUMBIA PICTURES INDUSTRIES, INC.

Lunchtime concerts by GERALD SHAW
on the Mighty Compton Organ at the
ODEON Leicester Square
Each Wednesday, at 12. 30 p.m.
Please Telephone Theatre for further information.

Admission 15p

Above: The Duchess.
Right: What a touch of class!
Far right: World Premiere, A Touch of Class, June 1973.

—Champagne and Party Time—

W hen *A Touch of Class* starring Glenda Jackson and George Segal was due to be released in June, Brut Productions were keen to make the premiere an extra special occasion. They supplied bottles of champagne

Programme

8.55 p.m.

The Band of the Royal Regiment of Artillery
The Herald Trumpeters of the Royal Regiment of Artillery

By kind permission of the Officers of the Royal Regiment of Artillery

Conducted by Major Robert Quinn, M.B.E., L.R.S.M., p.s.m.
Director of Music Royal Regiment of Artillery

9.20 p.m.

GOD SAVE THE QUEEN
THE NATIONAL ANTHEM OF THE UNITED STATES OF AMERICA

9.25 p.m.

A Touch of Class AA

11.10 p.m.
On Stage MISS GLENDA JACKSON
Introduced by MR. ERIC SYKES

The Band of the Royal Regiment of Artillery
The Herald Trumpeters of the Royal Regiment of Artillery
The Choir of Students from the Royal College of Music
with another
TOUCH OF CLASS

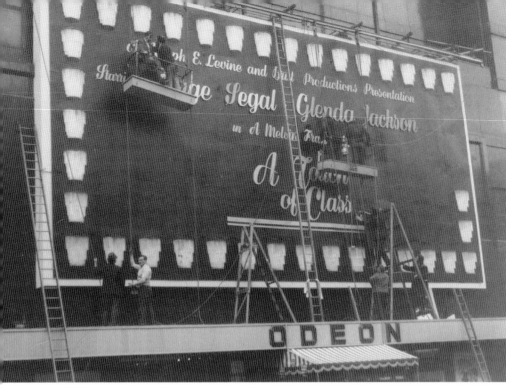

so that every member of the audience could have a glass of bubbly in the twenty-minute intermission. I was based at the large white reception desk on its platform in the middle of the main entrance foyer with two of our assistant managers, and plenty of champagne glasses and bottles. We poured out as many glasses as the desk top would accommodate, but there were one thousand people inside in the stalls! The doors opened. People poured into the foyer. Giving out full glasses cleared the desk pretty fast. There was no way we were going to be able to give out a thousand glasses in those twenty minutes, but we did our best! I kept pouring and passing, while the other two sat on the platform below me, opening more bottles. Every one of those bottles exploded! After all they had been carried out only a short while before,

and bounced, and slightly warmed by the foyer temperature – a definite recipe for excessive effervescence! But what was worse, because I was standing up on the platform, and the chaps were sitting on the step below me, every single bottle burst into life up my skirt! When the interval was over, I was absolutely awash with champagne! We each had a glass to celebrate our achievement, but actually when I felt my skirt, I knew I could wring it out and get a dozen more glasses out of it! There's nothing quite like being bathed in champagne!

There were many more bottles still unopened downstairs and there were loads of them left from the upstairs arrangement too, so when the evening was over, and we could finally close the doors and relax, the managers all sat down in the Royal Retiring Room and drank nothing but champagne! The film really did have *A Touch of Class* for us!

Below: Glenda Jackson arriving.
Near right: Sir Laurence Olivier.
Middle right: Sir Richard Attenborough.
Far right: Eric Sykes.

Above: July 1973, Bond is back! The Royal Premiere of
Live and Let Die.
Right: David Bowie and his wife Angela.

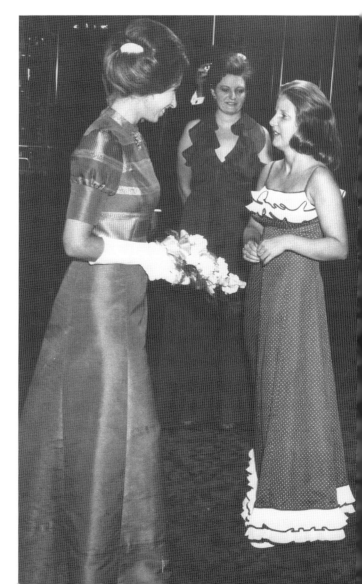

Left: Gregory Peck and his wife Veronique.
Bottom left: David Frost and Diahann Caroll.
Below: Princess Anne receives her bouquet.

It was 1973. A new Bond was about to arrive! Roger Moore! On Thursday 5th July Princess Anne came to the World Premiere of *Live and Let Die* at the Odeon. The evening raised £62,000 for charity – that's £659,000 in 2020! Lots of famous faces were there, Roger Moore of course, Burt Reynolds, Gregory Peck, Michael Caine, Paul McCartney, Bowie, Peter Sellers, David Frost, Lulu... The next day seven thousand, one hundred people came, including King Constantine of Greece, and the Saudi Prince Feisal. The abolition of the Greek monarchy happened that year. Two years afterwards Prince Feisal assassinated the Saudi King and was executed.

On its first weekend, *Live and Let Die* was unbelievably busy, with some people even threatening murder if they didn't get in! Business was amazing – in the first six days we had forty thousand admissions, taking £36,644.00 net – the equivalent today of £446,094.00. It was a new all-time cinema record for the whole country.

The following week Bond continued attracting huge numbers. The constant conversation and announcements to keep the foyers moving were tough on the voice box! The producer Cubby Broccoli was haunting the theatre, absolutely delighted by the crowds. On the Tuesday night there was a late showing after the ordinary evening house, a Charity performance again, with more famous faces – Barbra Streisand, Ernie

Left: Roger Moore.

Eon Productions Ltd.

DIRECTORS:
HARRY SALTZMAN
ALBERT R. BROCCOLI, U.S.A.
STANLEY SOPEL
R.A.Barkshire

2, SOUTH AUDLEY STREET,
LONDON
WIY 5DQ

TELEPHONE:
01-493 7953
CABLES: TILNEYFILM LONDON, W.I.
TELEX NO. 27682

ARB/jdw   July 19, 1973

Mr. John Thompson
The Manager
Odeon Theatre
Leicester Square
London, W.1.

Dear Mr. Thompson,

I want you to know how delighted Harry Saltzman
and I are with the success of "LIVE AND LET DIE" at
the Odeon Leicester Square Theatre. I also want you
to know how much we both appreciate the hard work and
enterprise of you and your staff in creating a new
box office record for your theatre.

Please accept the enclosed cheque for £250 as a
gesture of our appreciation. We will leave it up to
you to apportion this sum between yourself and your
staff as you deem appropriate.

Kindest regards.

Sincerely yours,

A. R. Broccoli

Enc.

The Producers are pleased.

Wise, and the Duke and Duchess of Bedford, the couple who had opened up Woburn Abbey to the public and created Woburn Safari Park.

Everyone was so delighted with the success, it was decided there should be an afternoon party in the Royal Retiring Room for the Reception staff who were putting in so much effort. And Roger Moore himself was coming!

It was an amazing gathering. Because of the level of afternoon business upstairs in the theatres, there had to be a kind of rota for the staff. That was fine. No one would miss out. It allowed everyone on the Reception staff to enjoy the moment, and to pose for staff photographs, to be introduced to the man himself, and have a conversation with this new attractive James Bond. The only trouble was everyone seemed to go shy! They stood in little groups, smiling and sipping a glass of bubbly and looking in awe at Roger Moore, but most of them not really feeling able to have a conversation with him – our confident, attractive and efficient staff, who could deal with thousands of people! Poor man was stuck with me! I had been given the brief to run the party and make sure all the staff enjoyed being celebrated, but much as I tried to introduce them to him, I couldn't find many who were brave enough to do more than meet him, smile, say just a few words and get his autograph. I have to admit I had a lovely afternoon talking with him about the theatre and the crowds coming to the film, and the numbers, and how we had broken all the records. Even that day the records were being broken! It was a real pleasure for me to meet such a charming man who could so happily chat to anyone!

performances of Chinese language films, which were very well attended because London's China Town was so near.

On 3rd December Princess Alexandra came to the premiere of the film *40 Carats*.

On December 11th we put on a champagne and smoked salmon 'do' for Herbert Wilcox to present to charity the £25,000 (nearly £310,00 today) achieved at that special November performance of *Sixty Glorious Years*. On 12th December, with all sorts of strikes starting and the Stock Market plunging, John and I were invited to the Cinema Exhibitors Association Ball at the Savoy. Very dressy! And there was another very important premiere due the following day!

On 14th November 1973, Princess Anne married Mark Phillips, and on 22nd of that month, the Queen Mother and Princess Alexandra came to the Royal Gala Performance of *60 Glorious Years*. The original film had been shown at the Odeon on October 14th 1938 in the presence of HM Queen Mary. Anna Neagle, who had played Queen Victoria in the film, went on stage to welcome the Queen Mother and Princess Alexandra to this performance. The following day there was an afternoon reception for the film's producer Herbert Wilcox, and all the West End Managers came.

That month *The Belstone Fox* starring Bill Travers had its premiere in the Odeon, and the first of what became regular Chinese shows began – late night

Far left: Raising a glass to all the hard work.
Bottom left: Roger Moore at our staff party.
Left: Roger Moore and Felicity.

In The Gracious Presence of

Her Majesty Queen Elizabeth
The Queen Mother

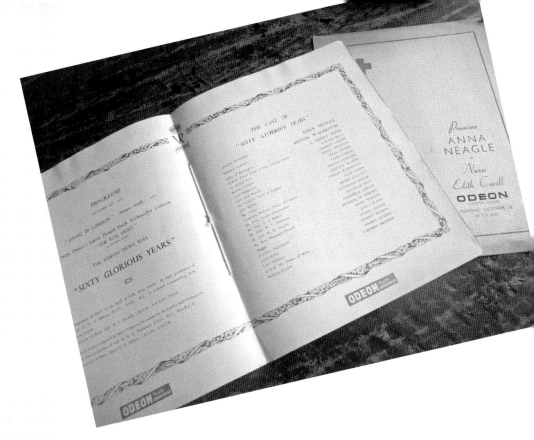

ROYAL GALA PERFORMANCE OF

Sixty Glorious Years

in aid of

King Edward VII's Hospital for Officers (Sister Agnes)
and Imperial Cancer Research Fund

ODEON THEATRE, LEICESTER SQUARE

THURSDAY 22nd NOVEMBER, 1973

—Tea for One and Fortnum Cakes—

Far left: The Royal Gala Performance of Sixty Glorious Years in November 1973.
First shown at the Odeon in 1938.
Above left: The programme shows the original cast.
Below left: The Queen Mother receives her bouquet.

Designed for Royal use if there was an intermission in the film they were attending, the Royal Retiring Room had an inner room too, and a beautiful en-suite toilet, just in case a member of the Royal Family needed it. In spite of the fact every time we had a Charity or a film performance that a member of the Royal family came to, it was my job to set the en-suite up with a new towel from Fortnum and Mason, new soap, and make sure it was very ready, none of them ever used that toilet! Nor did they come down to the Royal Retiring Room, except once, on 13th December that year when Princess Margaret and her two sons came to see the Opening Performance of *Robin Hood*. Among the familiar faces were Marty Feldman, Lynsey De Paul, Julia Foster, Mark Lester and John Cleese. It was exciting that we were showing the Disney film that John and I had seen in development in Los Angeles.

I usually set up a bar in the Royal Retiring main room, but on this occasion, as it was an afternoon performance and there was an intermission, I was also providing afternoon tea. This time, as well as the best soap, the cakes had to be from Fortnum and Mason too! And the cups and saucers had to be beautiful. The only thing that wasn't beautiful, I thought, was the cup of tea I passed to the Princess. It looked like the worst cup of tea I had ever poured, but protocol demanded I give her the first one! Well, I thought, I don't have any choice! It's manners! She did manage to drink it! Luckily the two boys opted for lemonade. That was much easier!

Earlier, my usual job of guiding the child forward to present the bouquet in the upstairs foyer had gone slightly awry too! Little Martin Lucas waited with me beside the wonderful costumed characters – the Lion King, Yogi Bear, Robin Hood, and Mickey Mouse. Princess Margaret was wearing a dark red coat. Her Lady in Waiting was wearing a paler, more distinct creamy colour. When Princess Margaret had been around the line-up of Walt Disney Film guests, she turned towards us. I had been whispering to little Martin about how pretty the Princess looked in red, and look, she's wearing a red coat, and encouraging him to be brave. He stepped forward, went straight past the Princess, and happily stepped up to the Lady in Waiting! I had to retrieve him and turn him back towards the Princess, so that the bouquet could be delivered into the right hands!

The following day there was a morning Trade Show for the film, followed the next morning by a Disney Children's party. And the film was taking good money. To keep up, I was back doing usheretting and seat counts with the other girls. A few days later there was a press show for *The Day of the Dolphin* at the LST, and late night, the staff did their annual pantomime in the circle lounge there, which was always marvellous. It inevitably ended up with a party, and no one went home until about 5 a.m.! But they were all there next day as usual!

On 21st December a bomb went off in the doorway of the Pastoria Hotel, right next door to us at the Leicester Square Theatre, but round the corner in narrow St Martins Street. Luckily there wasn't too much damage for the hotel, and the theatre wasn't affected at all, but it was very, very close. Now we had to be even more careful with all our safety

House lights down – Christmas panto lights up!

checks and controls. On 23rd, three more bombs exploded in London, one of them just along from the Square, in the Cinecentre in Panton Street.

Meanwhile, because of the strikes, there were new laws coming in to limit industry to operating just three days a week, but cinemas were exempted. We were given a different timetable.

—Lights Out—

From 31st December through to 7th March 1974 the lights in Leicester Square were out. The strikes meant that the theatres could only operate daily three hours on and three hours off. By cutting the ads off the programme length, it was just possible to fit together two runs of the film into three hours – and on both sides of the Square of course. We started in the Odeon at 1.45 p.m. for three hours, closed for three hours, and started again at 7.45 p.m., with the LST running twenty minutes behind the Odeon timing as usual. We sold all tickets in advance, and then we could show people to their seats in darkness – by ordinary usherette torchlight. The electricity came on and we could immediately show the film. Then those people could exit – not through the main foyers, but through side exits while the house lights were up. As they did, the new audience came in through the front doors, to be seated as soon as possible. The film would run through again – just! There was a minute or so to spare. Any delay to the film starting was fatal. We had exactly fourteen minutes between showings of *Robin Hood* for the turn-around. *The Day of the Dolphin* in the Leicester Square Theatre was tight. There could be no time in between. We had to use the final credits and opening credits to do the audience change over. At the end, with the electricity due to go off, we were ready to show people out by torchlight. Then we had three hours off. It was all very tricky, but it worked. We could have four showings of the film – both theatres, both films.

There were railway strikes, and petrol was in very short supply. Leicester Square Gardens filled up completely with black rubbish bags, one end to the other, and up at least as high as six feet. *Robin Hood* was still doing good business, and the Square was still constantly full of people, but life in London wasn't easy. One bomb went off at Madam Tussauds, and then another at the Boat Show. The miners were on a go-slow, and millions were wiped off stock-market shares. In spite of everything, *Robin Hood* had taken £87,000 in four weeks – over £927,000 today.

A new film *Executive Action* opened at the Odeon while *The Day of the Dolphin* was still showing at LST. On 28th of January, still using the three hours on and three hours off rule, there was another middle of the night Boxing match in both theatres – Ali beat Frazier on points.

The miners voted to strike. A bomb killed eleven people on a bus. Prime Minister Heath called a general election for the end of the month. Meanwhile the new film *The Way We Were* starring Barbra Streisand and Robert Redford opened at the Leicester Square Theatre and took £2,153, nearly £23.000 in today's money, on its very busy first day, even with the limited showings. Two days later it took £3,450, but with a smaller main foyer than the Odeon's, sometimes it was difficult in the LST, given the electricity restrictions on the performance timings, to deal with the crowds. On February 11th the Disney film *Herbie* was premiered at the Odeon and went on to show at the Dominion, meanwhile on the other side of the Square *The Way We Were* went on setting new records in the LST.

Our organist Gerald Shaw died. The election ended up deadlocked. Four days later Heath resigned, and Harold Wilson moved into Downing Street. The lights of Leicester Square were back on now, and we were back to long, long days. Films that had been delayed opened. On March 12th there was a press show for *Papillon* starring Dustin Hoffman, and the film opened two days later in the Leicester Square Theatre, taking over £20,000 in its first week – a new record. In today's money that is £213,000! It was amazing then how new box office records came along all the time!

On March 20th, someone tried to kidnap Princess Anne in the Mall. Seeing her at so many Royal occasions at the theatres, I wasn't a bit surprised she came through it so bravely and well. On 21st of the month John and I moved house from Chiswick to Coulsdon.

Four days later on 25th, the Queen Mother and Princess Alexandra came the 1974 Royal Film Performance, *The Three*

THE ROYAL FILM PERFORMANCE

In the Gracious Presence of
Her Majesty Queen Elizabeth The Queen Mother
to aid the Cinema and Television Benevolent Fund
Odeon Theatre, Leicester Square, Monday March 25th. 1974

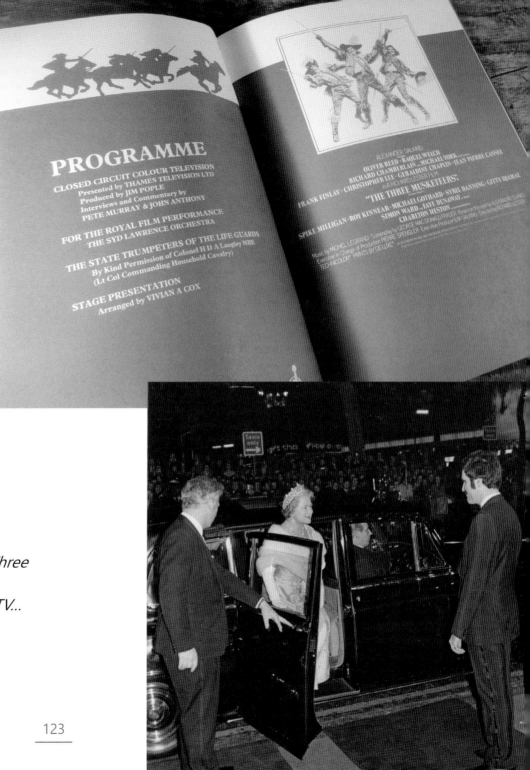

PROGRAMME

CLOSED CIRCUIT COLOUR TELEVISION
Presented by THAMES TELEVISION LTD
Produced by JIM POPLE
Interviews and Commentary by
PETE MURRAY & JOHN ANTHONY

FOR THE ROYAL FILM PERFORMANCE
THE SYD LAWRENCE ORCHESTRA

THE STATE TRUMPETERS OF THE LIFE GUARDS
By Kind Permission of Colonel H D A Langley MBE
(Lt Col Commanding Household Cavalry)

STAGE PRESENTATION
Arranged by VIVIAN A COX

ALEXANDER SALKIND
OLIVER REED · RAQUEL WELCH
RICHARD CHAMBERLAIN — MICHAEL YORK
GERALDINE CHAPLIN · JEAN PIERRE CASSEL
FRANK FINLAY · CHRISTOPHER LEE · a RICHARD LESTER FILM
"THE THREE MUSKETEERS"
SPIKE MILLIGAN · ROY KINNEAR · MICHAEL GOTHARD — SYBIL DANNING · GITTY DJAMAL
SIMON WARD — FAYE DUNAWAY
CHARLTON HESTON

Music by MICHEL LEGRAND · Screenplay by GEORGE MAC DONALD FRASER
Executive in Charge of Production PIERRE SPENGLER · Executive Producer ILYA SALKIND · Directed by RICHARD LESTER
TECHNICOLOR® PRINTS BY DE LUXE

*Left and above left: Royal Film Performance The Three
Musketeers, March 1974.
Above right: Orchestra, Trumpets, Closed circuit TV...
Bottom right: The Queen Mother arriving.*

HM The Queen Mother.

Above: Roger Moore and wife Luisa Mattiolli.
Right: Harold and Mary Wilson.

Thames Television

Thames Television Limited
Thames Television House
306-316 Euston Road
London NW1 3BB
01-387 9494

Mr. J. Thompson,   JP/MCC
General Manager,
Odeon Theatre,
Leicester Square,
London, W.1.   27th March 1974.

Dear John,

Thank you for your help and collaboration
on Monday's programme. It is generally
seen to be one of the best ones we have
done. I have asked Laurie to pass on
my thanks also to Mick and Jack and the
staff of the Odeon.

I will let you know when I can arrange
the usual playback for those who were unable
to see the transmission.

Yours sincerely,

JIM POPLE.

Musketeers. The usual filming of them arriving and meeting the stars and guests in the line-up was shown in colour for the first time on the screen inside the auditorium. Jim Pople at Thames Television was delighted with the results.

The Three Musketeers. film went on to be shown at the Carlton Cinema.

On 26th there was an evening Charity performance of *Papillon* starring Steve Macqueen and Dustin Hoffman, at the LST, while over the road, the film *Zardos* opened at the Odeon.

In May Assistant Manager Alan Jones and I began creating A2 posters for the LST Foyer, advertising things like the upstairs bar and special offers at the kiosk. It was really good fun and reminded me of how much I loved art, design and colour. I was also practising with fortune telling cards because there was a special event coming up in the summer for the Cinema and Television Benevolent Fund.

There was a morning press show for *Huckleberry Finn* on 2nd July, with Princess Margaret, and Princess Grace of Monaco at the premiere at the Odeon two days later. In its first four days the film only took £2500, and so the Saturday late night show was cancelled. Instead, on the Sunday night, nine hundred people came in to watch a Chinese film show. Three more Assistant Managers joined the management – more training for me to do!

On 13th July that year we went to the CTBF Garden Party at Glebelands in Wokingham. The Glebelands Care Home

Left: Thanks from Jim Pople at Thames TV.
Right: Dustin Hoffman with wife Anne Byrne.

Left: Princess Margaret arriving at the premiere of Huckleberry Finn, July 1974.
Right: Princess Grace of Monaco.
Below: A paired presentation.

was originally for people working behind the scenes in Cinema, film, and television, and was funded by the Cinema and Television Benevolent Fund, as it was called then. That Charity supported the annual Royal Film Performance and made a great deal of the money it needed from it. This garden party in the grounds and gardens of Glebelands was a nice opportunity to raise money ourselves directly for the cause. My idea proved very popular! I was dressed as a gypsy fortune teller with my own little tent, and once one person came in, shuffled the Tarot cards, and I dealt them out, and he sat listening just for the fun of it, he went out afterwards telling everyone about me. I must have told him something useful, because I suddenly had a long queue! The gates to the garden party were closing when I saw my last customer! It was great to be able to hand over the money to the cause.

When we had moved that summer, I went into the local bank in Coulsdon to open a new bank account and was appalled at the kind of reception I received. They were not prepared to take me seriously. I was a woman! I stayed with my old bank in Green Park.

On 17th July a bomb went off at the tower of London. A lot of people were injured and one person died. But London always went on being very busy. On 26th July the film *For Pete's Sake* opened at the Leicester Square Theatre. Over the previous thirty-two weeks, the Odeon and the LST had made a profit of £202,000. That is over two million pounds today. Even with the electric strikes and all the other problems, cinemas still took money.

A second general election looked likely in October, with Harold Wilson aiming to increase his majority.

On 1st August King Constantine of Greece came informally to the Leicester Square Theatre. John greeted him in the foyer and I showed the King and his party to their seats.

Later in August, the film *Caravan to Vaccares* opened at the Odeon with Princess Anne attending the Save the Children Charity performance. It was the first night back on duty for her bodyguard who had been wounded defending the Princess in the kidnap attempt on the Mall.

On 22nd August *The Tamarind Seed*, starring Julie Andrews and Omar Sharif opened at the Odeon, with a Calypso band playing in the foyer. Chinese late-night shows continued, and now there was talk of showing Italian football late on Sundays.

Gold opened on September 5th – Roger Moore acting in a non-Bond film, after all his success in *Live and Let Die*. At the premiere of this new film, Roger Moore was mobbed outside in the Square by the huge crowds – a popular man!

Left: The Royal Charity performance of Caravan to Vaccares,
August 1974.
Above: Princess Anne arriving.
Above right: Ready for the presentation.
Below right: The bouquet moment.

took £17,400 (£185,000 today) in its first five days, while *Juggernaut* which had been showing for twelve days, took £29,000 (the equivalent today of £309,000). Meanwhile there were strikes – lorry drivers, bus drivers, refuse men…

In those days the Royals would sometimes come informally to see a film. Princess Margaret came to see *The Odessa File*, entering and leaving the Odeon circle with John escorting her party through a side exit. And I remember having to ask a group of people in the Odeon front circle to move along the row when they were sitting in the wrong seat numbers. It turned out to be the Duchess of Gloucester and friends who needed to move along, but it was better to just smile and acknowledge her, once I recognised who she was, rather than make an obvious fuss of her. She was there privately, with no fanfare. Better for her to remain just one of the audience. She knew that too, and shot me a private smile as they moved along the row to the correct seat numbers.

Above: London Premiere of Juggernaut, October 1974.
Right: Princess Anne talks with Omar Sharif.

On October 10th the film *Juggernaut* premiered at the LST with Princess Anne and Mark Phillips there. At the end of the evening, after the front of house doors closed and the exits were locked, all the managers stayed on for a drink in the Odeon's Royal Retiring Room to hear the result of the general election. Harold Wilson won but with quite a small majority.

The film premieres went on. On 17th October at the Odeon when *The Odessa File* opened, I was operating a bar for Roger Moore and Harold Wilson! Both theatres were very busy. People needed cinema. *The Odessa File*

At the end of October of 1974 Princess Anne came to another Charity performance of *Juggernaut*. Twice to the same film for charity was really charitable of her! And then there was another late-night Boxing match beamed in with Ali beating Foreman in the eighth round with a knock out. The Odeon was knocked around too, as usual!

In late November the IRA was made illegal by Roy Jenkins and immediately reprisal bombs went off in pillar post boxes in Piccadilly and Victoria. And there was a bread strike! On 16th December the Queen and the young princes Andrew and Edward attended the premiere of the Disney film *Island at the Top of the World* at the Leicester Square Theatre. The figures for the end of the financial year in both theatres showed £315,000 profit, nearly five million pounds today! And in December James Bond would be coming back – *Man with the Golden Gun*, starring Roger Moore.

—Will It Be Forever?—

John and I were considering our future. With my level of energy and his business experience, it seemed to us we might go it alone, which was probably foolhardy given the country's financial condition. But why not? We bought a sandwich bar-cum-coffee shop in Bromley which I operated, while John stayed on in Leicester Square. Soon I was selling pizzas and jacket potatoes as well as sandwiches. I was busy! And closing at 6 p.m. every day gave me ample opportunity to come into Leicester Square to help on Charity or Royal Premieres! It was a strange mix on those occasions – finishing stacking the dishes, cleaning the shop floor, changing into evening dress, and driving into the West End, to be ready in the foyer to encourage people into the auditorium and manoeuvre the bouquet presenter into position! On the other hand, because I was up with the birds to open the coffee shop, if I didn't go into Leicester Square, or to the Cash and Carry for stock, I was home and in bed asleep long before John came home at midnight, or more often he was even later. We were hardly seeing each other. There had to be a better solution. After a few months we sold the shop and I went back to work for Rank while we looked for a new idea.

The Duke of Edinburgh came to the premiere of *Man with the Golden Gun* on 19th December and I came to help, bringing two of my lovely former shop girls, Connie and Jo, with me. They were thrilled to watch the line-up and see all the stars.

—A New Year—

At 11.45 p.m. on 31st December, John and I couldn't get the car out of the Odeon alleyway of course, so we joined the thousands of people in Trafalgar Square for the New Year celebrations. When Big Ben struck midnight, everyone was kissing the next person, and singing Auld Lang Syne, and the cars going past were all honking their horns! There were lots of police walking round, and since we knew some of them from Bow Street, it was too good an opportunity! I must have kissed a hundred policemen! Well, pecked! We were all laughing, and everyone was really happy and having fun. It was

Above left: Prince Philip jokes with Christopher Lee, Maud Adams and Roger Moore at the premiere of The Man with the Golden Gun, December 1974.
Right: A special presentation to the Duke.
Top right: The Royal World Premiere of Paper Tiger, David Niven and wife Hjördis Genberg.
Far right: David Niven with the Duke of Kent.

installing quadraphonic sound for the film *Tommy* due to premiere on 26th March.

Meanwhile on 17th March, the Queen came to the Royal Film Performance at the Odeon. Barbra Streisand, six years after she had played *Funny Girl*, was playing *Funny Lady*. She broke with protocol when she was introduced to the Queen and immediately asked Her Majesty why women had to wear gloves and men didn't at such royal occasions! Funnily enough, photos show James Caan next to her wearing gloves! There is still film of that evening on Facebook where Streisand is interviewed in the circle foyer and talks about being nervous at premieres, and more on YouTube of the Queen arriving wearing a beautiful peach coloured dress with sparkling diamond jewellery and tiara. Lots of stars came as usual, including Peter Ustinov, James Caan and James Stewart.

so nice just to be part of the crowd, rather than worrying about their welfare!

In January 1975 *Paper Tiger* starring David Niven had its Royal World Premiere at the Odeon, with the Duke of Kent there, and beautiful orchids passed out to the guests. On 12th of February Margaret Thatcher became the leader of the Opposition. In the Leicester Square Theatre electricians and sound men were working overnight every night

broadcast his show live from the foyer, with interviews with the guests. Ken Russell directed this amazing rock opera by the Who, and it won Rock Movie of the Year at the 1st annual Rock Movies Awards. The display advertising outside the theatre read: He Will Tear Your Soul Apart.

The film could certainly tear your ears apart! The quadraphonic sound was astonishing! If I had to walk across

At the beginning of April 1975 Mick McGloughlin was retiring. Projectionist for forty years, and for years Chief Projectionist in Leicester Square, he was formerly introduced that March to the Queen at the Royal Film Performance of *Funny Lady*, a very special honour, and then in April there was a special evening dinner at the Royal Garden Hotel in Kensington for him.

The Square was full of fans when the film *Tommy* opened at the Leicester Square Theatre on 26th March with stars Roger Daltry, Anne-Margaret, Oliver Reed, Tommy Steele, Eric Clapton, Ringo Starr, Rod Stewart with Britt Eckland, and Elton John, wearing his wonderful star-shaped glasses! There were special security guards on duty to protect the stars, and Capital Radio's Nicky Horne

Far left: The Royal Film Performance of Funny Lady, March 75.
Below left: Cecil Bernstein greets HM The Queen.
Left: James Stewart with wife Gloria and daughter Kelly.
Below: Barbra Streisand arriving.

the back stalls to reach the Ice-room, or the staff room, I had to put my hands over my ears to protect myself, and that was very far from being enough! I never did understand how the audience could sit through the enormous sound levels in the film, but the advance bookings were great, and from the first day on, there were huge sales of souvenir programmes, T-shirts and records at the kiosk, with chicken legs and a 'bubbly bar' upstairs at the Licensed Bar! The film set a new box office record for the LST, taking £26,978 in its first week – over £217,000 today.

More film premieres came all the time, including *Rollerball* in September at the Odeon with a special guest Ken Norton, the American Heavyweight boxer, and in December, the last month that John would be with Rank, *The Man Who Would*

Be King starring Michael Caine and Sean Connery opened at the Odeon.

John had decided the moment had come to leave. He had always been a star performer with Rank, winning sales and promotion prizes year after year, and overseeing huge box office success. Though there was a big farewell party planned by Head Office, there was definitely some doubt about whether John should be formerly introduced to the Queen or the Queen Mother, as Mick McGloughlin had been, to mark his retirement. But of course, John met the Royal family all the time! At every Leicester Square Theatre and Odeon Leicester Square Premiere, Royal performance, Charity Performance, and the annual Royal Film Performance, he was there on the red carpet to greet them, show them in, guide them up the stairs to the circle foyer, lead them inside their seats, show them out to their car at the end of the performance, and say goodnight. They knew him well, and were quite used to talking to him, and having him introduce them to other officials. But it seemed important to me that they should know he was retiring. After all they had shaken hands and smiled at him for years! Without telling anyone, I decided to write a personal letter to the Queen Mother to let her know. He had greeted her and so many members of her family on the red carpet for so long. Being the sweet woman she was, and giving him the recognition he fully deserved, and not mentioning me as I had suggested, John received a really lovely letter from her thanking him for his kindness to her and her family over the

years, and wishing him well. It was framed and has been up on our wall ever since. My letter to her has always remained a secret. Until now.

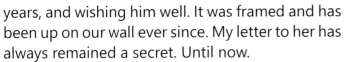

Left: At the Royal Film Performance of Funny Lady, Chief Projectionist Mick McGloughlin is presented to HM The Queen.
Above: Celebrating Mick McGloughlin – forty years as Chief Projectionist.
Above right: The British Premiere of Tommy, March 1975.
Right: Rod Stewart and Britt Eckland.

CLARENCE HOUSE
S.W. I

19th March, 1976

Dear Mr Thompson,

Queen Elizabeth The Queen Mother has learnt that you are retiring from the Rank Organisation, after 25 years, as the Manager of the Leicester Square and Odeon Theatres.

Queen Elizabeth remembers well the kindness you have shown her and other members of her family on their many visits to these two great theatres.

Her Majesty bids me say how much she appreciates your long and loyal service to the Rank Organisation, and sends you an expression of her warmest good wishes for the years ahead.

Yours
sincerely,

Comptroller to
Queen Elizabeth The Queen Mother

J. Thompson, Esq.

J. Thompson, Esq.,
30a Warwick Road,
Coulsden,
Surrey.

John

&

Felicity

Friday, 16th January 1976.

Guests of Honour - John and Felicity Thompson

Royal Roof Restaurant
Vendredi, le 16 janvier 1976

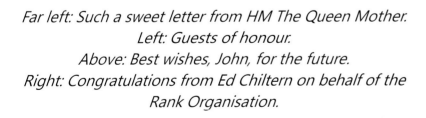

Far left: Such a sweet letter from HM The Queen Mother.
Left: Guests of honour.
Above: Best wishes, John, for the future.
Right: Congratulations from Ed Chiltern on behalf of the Rank Organisation.

—Different House Lights—

When John left the lights of Leicester Square, the two theatres were separated. No longer was there a Multiple Unit. John's good friend Alan Harris-Quelch who had been at the Dominion, became the manager at the Odeon, while Chris Hilton came to the Leicester Square Theatre from the Odeon Chelsea – and he eventually moved across the Square to the Odeon when Alan Harris-Quelch retired.

While John and I waited for our new venture, I worked instead in a whole new cinema world – the Rank theatres of South and West London. I had the grand title of Relief Manager, giving the actual manager an opportunity to have two consecutive days off. I worked at the Odeon Kensington which was part of the West End group of theatres, where the delightful Roy Pearce was General Manager, and a dear friend. Even though I was there to give him time off, he never took it, but I always got on well with him, doing any work he wanted me to. He was a hugely gifted pianist and at all the management parties he could play anything you suggested! He never needed a single sheet of music! Hum it and he'd play it! His lovely wife Eve had a superb voice too. Singing with the BBC choir, she knew every song in the book! I had worked at Kensington before helping on a couple of premieres, and it was the one and only place where I ever had to take a member of the Royal family to the Ladies. Princess Alexandra, and her Lady in Waiting, followed me up two staircases to the office washroom, and then down again, and were perfectly charming!

How different some of the theatres were. At Richmond, the Odeon was delightfully near the River Thames. Chris Hilton was there before moving to the Odeon Chelsea where I worked later that year. Chelsea Odeon was in the Fulham Road where the shops were all too tempting! Shepherd's Bush Odeon had a wonderful old painted sign on the side brick wall – I'm sure it was Stalls 1/6 – one shilling and sixpence – about £2.34 in today's money! Then there was the Odeon Peckham where the stock room always seemed to have been broken into. Crossing the road late at night there to the bank Night Safe with the takings, and parking by a dark rear exit where local young boys used to laugh and kid me they were dangerous was certainly fun! They weren't dangerous at all. I could talk them round and we could have a laugh together. I'd met boys just like them at the Leicester Square late night Boxing shows!

By the time I worked at the Odeon Wimbledon, the weather was boiling hot. 1976 was the year of the long heat wave, and people came to the movies to cool off in the air-conditioned auditorium! The Croydon Odeon was right in the middle of the shopping centre and was always very busy. At the Odeon Hounslow, the planes were going over into Heathrow every three or four minutes and the noise and vibration from them was so loud, it flattened the sound track of the film!

Far left: Raising a glass to our future together.
Left: Behind Felicity is Roy Money who first introduced them.

—Times Change—

Finally in January 1977, John and I moved to our perfect business, very far from the lights of London, on the beautiful and sunny Isle of Wight. We took out a mortgage to do it – at the going business borrowing rate of two per cent over the base rate, which was fifteen per cent at the time! Seventeen per cent! Over the next years on the Island, we were still dealing with the public – and very, very busy! Our holiday flats complex was fully booked summer after summer, but there was still the opportunity every year in early spring and late autumn to welcome all the West End managers for a weekend with us, and we never lost touch with all the London friends we had made, and right through the years, John continued to visit his other family frequently. I wish I had been allowed to meet them.

Inspired by the funny little cine-reel I had bought when John and I had been in California, I went on to write and produce fourteen travel films for tourists to buy and take home with them! On the beautiful Isle of Wight, we had sunshine instead of spotlights, and a leading lady in our little daughter, and a totally different way of life.

Years later in December 2000 when John died, my daughter and I were able to hold a party in the Royal Retiring Room in the Odeon Leicester Square so that the Reception and Box office staff who had worked with us, the West End Managers, and old Rank Organisation friends, could all come together to remember those wonderful days. When it got dark and the West End was lighting up, we all went up to the roof, way up, above the huge advertising hoarding. Even then, my daughter and I had to climb a ladder to get to the very top to see over into the Square.

There, as all his friends clapped, and remembered him, our daughter and I scattered John's ashes – out across the lights of Leicester Square.

—Odeon Theatres Today—

Times have changed from the days of J Arthur Rank and the Rank Organisation.

In July 2016 Odeon Cinemas was bought by the American company AMC Theatres.

Combining Europe and the UK at last count, the Odeon Cinemas Group has 3860 screens, and is the largest cinema operator in Europe. The group is a wholly owned subsidiary of AMC Theatres which, after acquiring Odeon Cinemas, Hoyts in Australia, and adding the European UCI Cinemas, and American Carmike Cinemas in the same year, became the largest movie theatre chain in the world with nearly 11,000 screens. AMC Theatres itself is owned by the Chinese Wanda Group, a multinational conglomerate with its headquarters in Beijing. The Wanda Cultural Industry is one of China's cultural enterprises which includes sports assets, and movie theatres and film production assets, making it the highest revenue generating film company in the world. Overall, the Wanda Group, through all its subsidiaries, has huge worldwide interests in sports, entertainment, media, industrial manufacturing, financial services, high technology, hospitality, real estate development, healthcare and retail.

—FILMS Featured—

Smashing Time	December 1967	Last Valley	April 1971
Romeo and Juliet	March 1968	Carnal Knowledge	September 1971
The Charge of the Light Brigade	April 1968	Bedknobs and Broomsticks	October 1971
Oliver	September 1968	Nicholas and Alexandra	November 1971
Shalako	December 1968	Diamonds Are Forever	December 1971
Chitty Chitty Bang Bang	December 1968	Mary Queen of Scots	March 1972
Funny Girl	January 1969	Kidnapped	May 1972
The Prime of Miss Jean Brodie	February 1969	How to Steal a Diamond	June 1972
Sweet Charity	February 1969	Young Winston	July 1972
McKenna's Gold	March 1969	Heist	September 1972
Ring of Bright Water	April 1969	Travels with My Aunt	February 1973
Run Wild Run Free	June 1969	Lost Horizon	March 1973
Batttle of Britain	September 1969	A Touch of Class	June 1973
On Her Majesty's Secret Service	December 1969	Live and Let Die	July 1973
Marooned	January 1970	60 Glorious Years	November 1973
Anne of 1000 Days	February 1970	The Belstone Fox	November 1973
Secret of Santa Vittoria	June 1970	40 Carats	December 1973
Cromwell	July 1970	Robin Hood	December 1973
Sunflower	August 1970	The Day of the Dolphin	December 1973
Too Late the Hero	August 1970	Executive Action	January 1974
Waterloo	October 1970	The Way We Were	February 1974
Tora Tora Tora	October 1970	Herbie	February 1974
The Private Life of Sherlock Holmes	December 1970	Papillon	March 1974
Murphy's War	February 1971	The Three Musketeers	March 1974
Love Story	March 1971	Zardos	March 1974
When Eight Bells Toll	March 1971	Huckleberry Finn	July 1974

For Pete's Sake	*July 1974*
Caravan to Vaccares	*August 1974*
The Tamarind Seed	*August 1974*
Gold	*September 1974*
Juggernaut	*October 1974*
The Odessa File	*October 1974*
Island at the Top of the World	*December 1974*
Man with the Golden Gun	*December 1974*
Paper Tiger	*January 1975*
Funny Lady	*March 1975*
Tommy	*March 1975*
Rollerball	*September 1975*
The Man Who Would Be King	*December 1975*

—Index of photographs—

Other books by Felicity Fair Thompson
The Kid on Slapton Beach
Cutting In
Hold Tight

Stage Plays
Exit the King
Voices Over Passchendaele

Children's Stories
Hugo the Hungry Pig
The Concert Party
Grandpa's Dear Old Girl
Chrissy and the Sea Witch (coming 2022)

Films
The Beautiful Isle of Wight
The Isle of Wight – A Closer Look
Fairest Isle
PS Waverley – The Little Paddle Steamer and the Great White Whale
Ventnor Botanic Garden
A Feather for the Crown
Carisbrooke Castle – 1000 Years of British History